# YOU:
# A Spiritual Being on a
# Spiritual Journey

.......

*A New Paradigm for Living Life*

Dear Sophia,

Your Self is at
home — here in connect,
listen, Trust & Act,
Step in boldly —
Let your True Self
awaken to the
Journey You chose
this lifetime.

With love, Andrew

# YOU:
# A Spiritual Being on a
# Spiritual Journey

.......

*A New Paradigm for Living Life*

INDIRA DYAL-DOMINGUEZ

TURNING
STONE
PRESS

First published in 2014 by
Turning Stone Press, an imprint of
Red Wheel/Weiser, LLC
With offices at:
665 Third Street, Suite 400
San Francisco, CA 94107
*www.redwheelweiser.com*

ISBN: 978-1-61852-080-7
Cover design: Jeff Clapp

Printed in the United States of America


IBT
10 9 8 7 6 5 4 3 2 1

*To Paul:*

*You have my heart*

# Contents

# Prelude

This book is written from the communication that dwells within each of us: that dimension of ourselves that exists within us but which we have not had access to from the current paradigm of life. Some of us call it intuition, our gut instinct. In this book we will look at this dimension of our *Self* such that it becomes a real tool in living our lives for what we know our "Soul" is here to experience.

# Introduction

YOU: *A Spiritual Being on a Spiritual Journey: A New Paradigm for Living Life* is a book about knowing yourself, not just as a mind and a body, but as an eternal spirit or *Self*, a vibration that is eternal. More importantly, this book is about being able to communicate with that eternal *Self* in a way that allows you to complete the journey you are here in this lifetime to fulfill. It teaches you how to Connect to the *Self* and how to use such connections to live a satisfying and fulfilling purpose-driven life.

In the current paradigm, people turn to their *Mind* for the answers to everything. There's nothing wrong with that. However, the *Mind's* energy and vibration are all about survival, which does not allow for a calming, peaceful way of living. The *Mind's* design is to keep us constantly worried about the future and regretful about the past, without letting us be in the present or in a moment of "now." This book is about establishing a new paradigm in which you can Connect to your *Self* for the answers that are unique to you that will unfold the journey YOU are here to fulfill. Connecting to your *Self* provides the answers to live a better life, as well as allowing for a peaceful, stress-free way of experiencing that life.

YOU: *A Spiritual Being on a Spiritual Journey* provides the tools for you to distinguish between the *Mind's* energy and the *Self's* energy, allowing you to access your *Self* at will. This book includes specific exercises so that readers can immediately start to get results for themselves. These tools are what distinguishes this book from many others in the self-help field. By doing the exercises, the reader will shift from relating to life from their *Mind* to experiencing it from their *Self*, and a new opening arises from which to resolve the issues that keep us stuck in life.

YOU: A *Spiritual Being on a Spiritual Journey* also shares anecdotal stories from people who have experienced Connecting to their *Self* and getting the answers and actions to take to produce positive outcomes in all of the most important areas of life, such as relationships, finances, work/business, health issues, and more. These are the stories that will inspire you to use the same tools to Connect, Listen, Trust, and Act.

## How This Book Came About

I was never fulfilled by whatever I was doing. It was great that I was making a good living as well as making a difference in people's lives, but somehow it was still not the answer. I knew that the life I was experiencing was not what truly fulfilled me, and as such, it always felt like I didn't belong, no matter where I was or what I was doing. I wanted to live my life with being fulfilled as my number-one purpose. I pursued many different journeys of inner growth as well as many different philosophical and spiritual things, and yet I still did not get the answers I was looking for.

YOU: A *Spiritual Being on a Spiritual Journey* emerged as I sat in my room, knowing that I had come to a place in my life where I could no longer do anything unless it fulfilled my life's purpose. With no understanding of what that meant, but knowing it was the only way to move on in my life, day after day I sat in quiet and silence, turning within. Suddenly one day I began to experience a stirring inside, a "knowing" that resonated with a truth that I embraced. I knew unconditionally that this was the vibration of my spirit, my *Self*—what I had been seeking all my life. I felt its love and presence as a peace that transcended all that was of the physical dimension.

As I began Connecting to the *Self* within, a clear communication arose through four simple steps of Connecting, Listening, Trusting, and Acting. With these four steps anyone can live life from a place that honors the journey their *Self* is here to unfold.

I started by holding workshops in which I facilitated others in Connecting to their *Self*. I still teach these workshops, as well as other individual and group webinars and programs. I also work with my husband, who is a business consultant, to bring these tools to high-level corporate executives. I have been running these programs for the past fifteen years. However, the next action I was called to in Connecting to my *Self* was to write books to reach a larger audience and provide the tools to allow for more people to begin the practice of Connecting to their *Self*.

## What I Hope to Provide

YOU: *A Spiritual Being on a Spiritual Journey* will give you the ability to find personal answers to live a better and more fulfilling life. By distinguishing between the *Mind* and the *Self*, this book provides specific tools that anyone can use to access their intuitive *Self* and to live their life from a new paradigm. In using these tools many people are finding the answers to their most important questions and putting those answers into practice to live a more satisfying, stress-free, and peaceful life.

Most people today live life through the predominant cultural paradigm of listening to the *Mind*, only heeding what their *Mind* tells them is real. This leaves them stressed out, concerned, and worried about everything from their personal finances to global warming. While there are many tools out there for people to use to feel better, those tools may not shift them out of their *Mind's* view of life. The impact is that people are left feeling like they can do their very best, but never be fulfilled in what they know they are capable of doing, and never experiencing what their purpose in life is.

Simply by reading this book and recognizing that there is a *Self* you can turn to that will provide the answers you need, your vibration actually shifts from the current paradigm into the new paradigm where Connecting, Listening, Trusting, and Acting from the *Self* become a natural way of living.

Many of the self-help books out there are written mainly as philosophies which could be difficult to conceptualize and may not speak to a broad audience. Many of these books lack clear personal tools and methods for people to get the answers they are looking for to live a fulfilled life. This book provides clear access to answers to live a life from your *Self*.

You will not simply read the book; there are actual exercises for you to practice Connecting to your *Self*. The act of Connecting actually shifts your vibrational energy so that you will have an experience of knowing your *Self*. *YOU: A Spiritual Being on a Spiritual Journey* is the next level in self-help, providing actual personal tools versus just philosophy and guidance for real attainable results.

What is different in this book is that it creates a new paradigm driven by the *Self* instead of the *Mind*. By providing you with answers that will let you know that you are honored and cared for, no matter what is occurring, you will be assured that what is going on in your life is part of your journey. It will give you actual results and a deep knowing that you are fulfilling what you are on the planet for in this lifetime. This in turn will provide you with a level of peace you have never felt before.

# How to Read This Book

*We are all on a spiritual journey.* Knowing this truth has led you to hold this book in your hands. This book begins, not with the reading of it, but rather by knowing holding it is a function of how you resonate and vibrate. This is a new reality: to know that what is occurring around us and what is happening in our lives is a function of the energy in which we vibrate and the frequency in which we resonate.

As you read this book, you will experience a shift in awareness from the current paradigm of the *Mind* to a new paradigm of your *Self*. This journey will unfold a new context for you, as you bring your awareness to knowing your *Self*, as YOU, and as you begin to relate to your *Mind* as a dimension of you, not all of who you are.

You may find yourself struggling with the *Mind's* view of what is being said, but as you slow down life and begin to allow your *Self* to arise, all of what is written will begin to resonate as your own truth, that of your "inner knowing." It will begin to resonate as what you have been seeking, but never had the language to express or a new paradigm in which to experience this You of your higher *Self*.

Each section is designed to evoke another energy and vibration of your *Self*.

In the Conception chapter you will have a shift in the context of your life from your *Mind* as You to your *Self* as You.

In the Current Paradigm chapter you will discover the *Mind's* role in the journey of your *Self*. You will achieve a depth of knowing the *Mind* as a tool for the journey of You.

In the New Paradigm chapter you will discover the depth and breadth of your *Self*. You will access a new reality of life where living from your *Self* is the journey You came here to experience.

In the Connect chapter you will activate the Connection to the *Self* and know that when you Connect you will have access to your *Self* as naturally and effortlessly as you do with your *Mind*. You will be able to Connect to your *Self* at will.

The Listen, Trust, and Act chapters will move you further into the new paradigm of your *Self* as who you are. In each chapter you will have a personal experience of how every step relates to situations in your life., You can begin to apply these steps to your own life situations.

In the Death chapter you will transcend the fear of the *Mind*, releasing the current paradigm as your truth and embracing a new paradigm of *Self* as your journey. The new reality will come alive as a dimension that is now here for a life that fulfills who you are and why you are here.

The final chapter, YOU, is a guide to being on your journey, having your actions in your life come from your *Self*. When you have a new awareness that you are not your *Mind*, you can begin to Connect, Listen, Trust, and Act from your *Self*, thus shifting from the concerns of the *Mind* to a "knowing" of your *Self* as you walk your life's journey.

Take time to read each section. Do the exercises, using the web links, that are designed to deepen your experience of what is being shared.

Each person will experience this as a journey that is unique to every individual. The glossary at the end of the book clarifies the meaning of the words we will use in the context of this conversation.

Feel free to keep a notebook or journal nearby to write what may be opening up or occurring for you. In fact, I encourage you to write down what you get from the exercises and from Connecting to your *Self* in chapter nine, YOU: Living Your Journey . . . Now. As you are reading, don't relate to what is shared as merely information, allow it to evoke the vibration of your highest *Self*.

There is only one experience you are here for—to honor the true journey of your *Self*.

A new world will emerge as you begin to have your life unfold from your *Self*, allowing you to finally experience the gift of life as it was designed—to be a vehicle for experiencing your true and divine nature in a physical form.

When the light within you is alive with its truth, as you Connect, Listen, Trust, and Act from your *Self*, distinct from your *Mind*, you will be within the joy and fulfillment of the You that came into being for a remarkable experience.

# ✐ 1 ✑

# Conception: The Journey
# of *Self* Continues

Conception is the fusion of YOU, with a *Body* and a *Mind*. You made a choice to once again be in a *Body* and have a *Mind* so that YOU can experience your magnificence. Relating to the truth of this statement shifts the entire context of your life. This is because it gives you an understanding of yourself as an eternal vibration of energy and divine "knowing."

What I am saying here does not resonate in our daily knowing from our *Mind* because it is too disruptive. However, for our *Self* we are a vibration of energy that houses our divine "knowing" of all that exists and all that is embodied in the universal consciousness. It is this You that chose to enter a physical form. When you can accept an awareness of this truth, you can begin to allow your true *Self* to exist separate from how your *Mind* is designed and relate to who you really are.

## You Embody within Your DNA a "Knowing" of Who You Are and Why You Are Here

Your energetic vibrational force of energy and consciousness houses within its resonance your true essence: who you are as your divine *Self*. Your true being is this energetic vibrational resonance that is energy. It is this energy that flows through your *Body* resonating and vibrating in your DNA. As your *Self*, your DNA vibrates with those truths that align with your true *Self*. It is this "knowing" that we sometimes feel within us but have no way to tune into or to bring into being, because from our *Mind* this dimension of us is not part of the physical experience of life. We sometimes call this "knowing" an intuition or a gut feeling. The "knowing" that vibrates within us, in our DNA, is a vortex, a source of all there is to know in any moment of "now," that would have us be related to what is there from our true and highest *Self*. A moment of "now" is when you are completely present and alive to whatever is happening in that instant with no thoughts about past situations, no worries about future situations, and no filtering or commenting by the *Mind* on what is going on. It is simply being in the experience that is occurring.

This "knowing" is the eternal You, your spirit, what we are calling your *Self*. This "knowing" is what is real. It is You. It is the You of your true *Self*. It is the part of you that chose to be here for a remarkable experience, such that whatever you do in this life comes from this "knowing." Your "knowing" is the eternal part of you. It is your spirit. It is your true nature. It is the part of you that allows your life to unfold peacefully, effortlessly, and naturally in the face of all of what the physical world throws at you. It is the dimension of you that transcends the physical realm to activate an energy that allows you to be in the world—but not of the world. It is the "knowing" of your true nature, your spirit called your *Self*. This is what is always resonating with the truths that allow you to live from your true *Self*.

## Why My *Self* Chose to Be in This *Body* for This Lifetime

Like many of you, there have been times in my life when I experienced the vibration of "knowing," and felt the vibration of my *Self*, and also many times when I longed to know who I was and why I was here. I recall a feeling of being disconnected from the world around me as a child. I remember thinking: "These are my *earthly* parents." I always had a strong desire to know who I am and why I am here even from a young age.

I lived within an experience of wondering and searching for the true Me that I knew was there but did not know how to get to. What seemed even more puzzling is that the world around me did not seem to have any connection to this Me. I instinctively knew that this Me was not somewhere around myself, but I was not sure how to find this part. I clearly knew that being this Me was why I was here, and there was no point to being here if I couldn't be true to that "knowing." These feelings, while dormant during some of my early years, stayed alive within me, and as such, my life unfolded in what was more of a seeking and searching to get to Me.

The core of my life became this seeking to discover more about my relationship to life—why I was here and what there was for me to do while I was here. Always in the foreground was a clear "knowing" that being here was somehow not about all the ordinary stuff that life consisted of for most people.

After having the experience of being very successful in my life, I found myself still on this quest. Even though I had a job in which I made a difference and a positive impact for many people, I still felt disconnected. I experimented with many different transformational courses and spiritual disciplines, and while most of them provided a level of fulfillment, they still did not provide the experience of being in touch with this Me that I knew was there. I was still feeling disconnected.

I knew deep within myself that I had come to a place where I could not continue to do something that still had me feel disconnected from Me. During this time, there was truly nowhere to turn—there was nothing in the world that I could step into that called for an experience where I felt I could be Me. No matter how much I tried to experience being Me with where I was and what I was doing, it did not feel right.

This was truly a dark time. I was in an experience that nothing in this world existed that called for me to be fully who I felt I was, yet not knowing what that meant. Nothing in the physical realm could fulfill or connect to or satisfy whatever this experience was that had resonated for me since I was a child. Any step I took into life would keep me on the same path where even the best of my self-expression was still not what I needed . . . I had no more answers, I had no more seeking, I had nowhere to go.

I left my career at that time as I continued to seek for this feeling within of disconnection. Not knowing where to go, I found myself sitting by myself. I knew from within there was nothing and nowhere to turn to in life.

It was in this place, on a day just like every other day, that a profound experience occurred when I Connected to the energy and vibration of what I now know to be my *Self*.

I experienced this part of me not as a dimension of my *Mind*, but *void* of my *Mind*.

I experienced a force of consciousness so strong and so clear and so powerful it became my reality.

My *Mind* stepped back as I experienced the energy and vibration of my true *Self*, my Higher *Self*. I experienced a Connection that allowed my *Self* to be in the here and now as real as the physical world around me. I experienced the depth and the breadth and the dimensions of this *Self* that transcends my physical *Body*, and my dominating *Mind*, with its eternal nature. I knew this force of energy as the Me I had been looking for; I felt its divine presence and eternal knowing that "spoke" to me. Its reality altered my relationship to who I was: I experienced myself as an eternal vibration of divine energy first, and then I experienced my *Body* as a vessel for my journey as a human being and my *Mind* in service of the journey of *Self*. This came to me in an instant, and in that moment I began to experience the energy of *Self* first, and the physical world around me second.

I knew in that moment that this was the ME that came here for this journey, and in that moment a paradigm shift occurred. I began to experience this dimension of myself as who I truly am and as what is real.

A new paradigm emerged. A new view of life unfolded. In that moment arose a clear "knowing" that when I Connect, Listen, Trust, and Act from my *Self*, I am honoring the Me that chose to be here for this experience. I realized my *Self* as separate and distinct from my

*Mind.* I experienced my *Mind* as a tool from which to live Me. I knew and understood that my *Self* is who I am and why I am here. I embraced the steps of Connecting, Listening, Trusting, and Acting as the journey that I am here to unfold and experience.

In that moment I knew that if all I did in my life was to live in the alignment and "knowing" of what there is to be in action about from my *Self,* my life would be what I came here to experience. And so I began my true journey.

Through Connecting, Listening, Trusting, and Acting from my *Self,* I began to lead workshops which shared this knowledge with others so they too can live life from their *Self* as who they really are.

Over the past fifteen years I have found a deep appreciation for the great ease, effortlessness, and peace that a human being can experience in their life through living from this new reality, this paradigm shift.

I have discovered through my *Self* a dimension of life where I have access to my *Body,* to healing myself, to experiencing, honoring my family, my partner, my friends, and life itself from a place that disconnects the fear, anxiousness, concern, and worry that prevails, and only heightens as we unfold life from our *Mind* as our only reality.

I have claimed the joy of why I chose to be here on this incredible journey called life. I am unfolding who I am and the expression of my life through stepping away from my *Mind* as who I am as I Connect, Listen, Trust, and Act from my *Self.*

I believe this is a new paradigm for humanity: a shift where living from our *Self,* distinct from our *Mind,* is a natural way to be. From this new paradigm life becomes about being our *Self,* and all that exists in the physical realm are tools for experiencing this life, for whatever time we are in our *Body*, where it is unquestionable that in each moment of "now" we are being our true *Self*. In this paradigm everything unfolds in the honoring of our *Self* and the *Self* of every person. This is why the Me I had been searching for all my life chose to come into life again.

## Your Choice to Be in a Human Form Is to Experience Your True *Self*

Who is the YOU that chose? Let's take a look at this example to get related to this YOU.

> Take a moment to reflect on a Body where the person has died. There is no pulse. There is no breath. There is no brain wave activity. What is that pulse, that breath, that brain wave activity? It is all energy. When someone has died, there is no flow of energy through the Body. We call this state flatlining. The person's Body is there, but we know right away that "they" are not. So we know we are not our Body because we bury or cremate the Body knowing that the Self that is YOU has left the Body.

You are an energetic vibrational force of divine consciousness. You vibrate and resonate with a "knowing" that you are eternal and that you are on an eternal journey. This eternal journey is you getting to experience life through your *Self*, given in a body you can experience your *Self* through the physical dimension. You can experience love, compassion, empathy, forgiveness, the knowing that "all is well"—all of what is real from the You of your *Self*.

This is why you were excited and passionate to be once again in a *Body*—to have the gift of being a human being. It is only through this gift you can know your *Self* and experience the deep and magnificent You.

## A Shift in Awareness Activates Your Journey

Your shift in awareness begins by distinguishing your *Mind* as separate from who you are. This is the awareness that activates a new paradigm: that you are not your *Mind*.

Remember that understanding this intellectually is still operating from your *Mind*. What is different here is to actually experience this shift in awareness as a way of living your life. The power here is that this becomes a new state of consciousness that allows you to live in the duality of your *Mind* as separate and distinct from your *Self*. In this energetic shift you will begin to vibrate and resonate as your true *Self*.

Here is an exercise designed to begin to open up this new awareness:

- Choose a situation in your life where you find yourself struggling, where you experience some turmoil or unknown in how to handle things to be fulfilled in that area. Now, take a moment to pause and close your eyes. Begin to listen to what your *Mind* has to say about that area. All of the thoughts and words you are hearing are your *Mind*. YOU are not those words and thoughts: that is your *Mind*. Observe these thoughts as your *Mind*. Listen to what is being said from the awareness that this is your *Mind*. *All* of it is the *Mind*.

- Now bring forth the awareness that you have a *Mind* and a *Self*. If you are observing your *Mind's* thoughts, then who is it that is doing the observing? It is your *Self*. It is another dimension of you that is as real as your *Mind*. Begin to relate to your *Self* as a new reality. In this moment you have brought forth an experience of your *Self* that is as real as your experience of your *Mind*.

• Now, imagine you can unplug your *Mind* and Listen to your *Self*. Keeping your eyes closed, listen again. Listen for the softer tone and vibration. Listen for what is present from your *Self* about the situation you've been struggling with. This *Self* is You. It is what is *real*. It is always in communication about what is occurring in all areas of your journey. It is the part of you that lives on after You have left your *Body*. Bring this awareness to the forefront as a truth. Allow yourself to be in the awareness of your *Self* as You.

• Now open your eyes and take a moment to journal what the *Mind* is saying and then journal what your *Self* is saying. You will be within the experience of the difference between the two. This is the awareness of the "knowing" of your *Self* as who you are. It is this *Self* that has fused with a *Body* and a *Mind* to experience a journey of knowing itself. You are now on a journey to experience your *Self* as YOU!

(To hear an mp3 audio of this exercise, go to www. indiratoday.com/Books/conception.)

(Note: The energy of the *Mind* sounds strong, logical, firm, loud, attached, and often contains words like *should* and *have to*. The energy of your *Self* sounds soft, loving, unattached, and is often presencing "all is well," "all is as it should be exactly the way it is.")

By simply doing this exercise, you have shifted your awareness to a new truth: that you are not your *Mind* and that YOU chose a *Body* and a *Mind* to experience your true *Self*.

## The Duality—Two Distinct Journeys Unfolding Simultaneously

On this journey that we chose, we live in the duality of living life from the *Mind* and from the *Self*. The "knowing" of our journey as a duality allows us to experience both the *Mind* and our *Self* as two separate and distinct energies. Without this distinction the *Mind* creates the feeling that its journey is the truth and is who we are. Creating a relationship that there is a duality is very powerful, for it presences the *Mind* as a *dimension* of who we are, *not* who we are.

In the next chapter on the current paradigm of the *Mind*, we will explore the depth and dynamics of how the *Mind* is organized to lead us to experience the *Mind* as our only reality.

The journey of your *Self* exists simultaneously with the journey of the *Mind*, and is on its own journey. The journey of the *Self* is a journey of being thrilled and excited to have this physical experience to know and to honor your *Self* and the *Self* of each person. How you can know your *Self* is to shift the *Mind* to be in service of the *Self's* journey. Living from your *Self* is to know and discover who you are and why you are here.

From within the journey of the *Mind* there is no existence of your *Self*. The *Mind* is set up to operate this way to ensure your survival. It is only in holding on to the duality that you can begin to presence a new paradigm for your life. In the "knowing" of your *Self*, distinct from the *Mind*, is a new state of being.

The following is designed to give you an experience of holding both the *Mind* and *Self* in duality.

> Take a moment to close your eyes. Take a deep breath. Now allow yourself to presence that you have a *Mind*, a *Body*, and a *Spirit*. Presence your *Spirit* as You—called your *Self*. Imagine that it is this You that chose to have a *Body* and a *Mind* such that You can know your *Self* as a divine being. This "knowing" is an energy that resonates within you, as You.
>
> Imagine the *Mind* as an energy that creates itself as You. Imagine living like you are your *Mind* when you are *not*. Bring forth an awareness that within the *Mind's* energy, your *Self* never gets to experience itself as real. Create for yourself the duality of your *Mind* as separate and distinct from your *Self*. Hold *both*. Your access to your *Self* lives in honoring the duality of *Mind* and *Self*.
>
> (To hear an mp3 audio file of this exercise, go to www.indiratoday.com/book/conception2.)

## The *Body*—A Vessel for the Journey

Your *Body* allows you a physical form in which to experience the journey of *Self*. The *Mind* has us relate to our *Body* as who we are. This is an illusion generated by the *Mind*. It keeps having you misidentify your *Body* as your *Self*. In the new paradigm, you will see your *Self* and then see your *Body*. This new view reveals a dimension of life that can heal your *Body*, as well as allow you to hear what is being evoked by your *Body* for what serves it best. From the perspective of your *Mind*, your *Body* is who you are;

from your *Self*, your *Body* is the vessel here to honor the journey of your highest *Self*.

With this shift in awareness, you begin to experience your *Body* as an energy that communicates its needs and what best serves your *Body* and honors it. Abusing your *Body* through the misuse of food, alcohol, drugs, and other addictions becomes impossible when you shift from what your *Mind* is evoking to what your *Self* is presencing.

### Getting Present to the *Body*

Close your eyes and take a deep breath. Release all of the *Mind's* thoughts. Now, presence your *Body* as a vessel for your *Self*—an eternal vibration of energy called You. With each breath imagine and presence the energy and vibration of You, as an eternal energy, in each cell. Presence the moment You chose to enter this journey at conception. The *Self* ignited the spark that formed the *Body* as a vessel for its vibration. Imagine, from your *Self*, the *Body* being honored for the intricate and exquisite way it works and functions. This is a new perspective from which to hold your *Body*. It is an energy that vibrates with the essence of your highest *Self*.

(To hear an mp3 audio file of this exercise, go to www.indiratoday.com/Books/conception3.)

## The "Set-Up"—Your Relationship with Parents, Family, Spouses, Partners, Siblings

Your conception was not arbitrary or random. You chose the parents and family you were born into—everything about your life was known to you as you chose to be conceived—your race, culture, nationality, etc., were all part of that choosing. Each situation that you find yourself in is designed to reveal something about your journey such that you can transcend the *Mind* to access your *Self*. In the experience of being a human being, and living from the *Mind* as our reality, we find ourselves dealing with our closest relationships from what gets triggered within us from our *Mind*.

These triggers are energies that are "set up" to disconnect us from our *Self*. It is not a mystery why things in our life are "set up" this way, but rather this journey has been designed this way when we have the *Mind* as separate from our *Self*. They are energies for us to move through and transcend to become more fully our *Self*.

Our parents, family, children, spouses, partners, and siblings evoke "karmic energies"—energies designed to keep us in an experience of ourself and life that is designed from the *Mind's* truth about who we are. In our journey with them these energies keep replaying themselves until we transcend them and are no longer triggered by them. In this "set-up" we are always confronting our *Mind's* truth about us and them. These energies are strong. The energy of the "set-up" is inescapable and has us confront what we might not normally choose to confront. Whether we confront it or not is a function of the *Mind*, but from the energy of our *Self*, it is why we are here. To transcend the energies and the *Mind's* truth is to have our actions come from our *Self*.

The gift we experience is to once again be able to honor our *Self* and their *Self*. It is here that we share in the joy of life.

**Ramonita, Social Worker**

I was living in Florida when I first started Connecting to my *Self*, and what came up was for me to go back to live in Puerto Rico with my family to help them. My mother was ill, and I got from my *Self* that I should be there. That was the first time I trusted completely what I got from my *Self*, so I moved back home.

When I came to Puerto Rico, I had it that I came to really help my parents and to take care of them—my mom more so than my dad. When my mom passed, I realized that my relationship with my mom was one journey, and the one with my dad is a totally different journey. The journey with my father is, in some ways, even more important than the journey with my mother was. I got from my *Self* that I was going to really have to fight tooth and nail to transcend the *Mindful* energies with my dad because they are very strong and have been with me for a lifetime. In taking care of my dad, I would find myself feeling like a child again many times, and not feeling like I was being heard or appreciated or acknowledged for being here to take care of him. Although I chose to do that from the heart, I still wanted to be acknowledged and honored for what I was doing for my father. And I always found it very difficult to have that with my dad. We finally came to a crossroads, but through Connecting, I was able to see that my being here is a "set-up" to transcend my *Mind* with my dad. It's not something that I feel is an obligation now, so I started to be able to share myself differently with my dad. I started to speak to him in a way that would generate conversations back from him that came from a whole different place. I became clear that I was the one making a difference for our relationship by coming from my *Self*, and our living together has been really great since I've been doing that. I now feel that my dad does appreciate me and honors who I am. Every now and then, I still have times when I feel myself react to the something he's done or said, but I see more quickly that that is my *Mind* making me think this way about him. Now I'm clear it's my *Mind*. But, when I Act from my *Self*, instead of reacting from my *Mind*, it's generated a relationship between the two of us that is really at a whole other place for the both of us—a place in which we both really honor each other. I've also become more clear that my dad has his own journey and I've got to let that one unfold on its own as I let my own journey unfold, as opposed to thinking that I'm responsible for his journey. No, he's got his own journey and I've got mine, and that's generated a whole other place for us to be with one another, and it's great.

The following exercise is designed to begin to presence our energy from our *Self*, distinct from our *Mind*, with the most important people in our lives:

Close your eyes. Take a deep breath and release the *Mind's* thoughts. Presence your parents, children, siblings, friends, partners, and spouses. As you continue to let go of the *Mind's* thoughts, bring forth the awareness that each person around you in your life is designed to evoke energies that disconnect you from being your *Self* with their *Self*. Picture each person individually and presence where there is a disconnect from love between the two of you. Notice the *Mind's* thoughts about this person. Choose to "see" this person through the view of your *Self*, not your *Mind*. Then bring forth the awareness and listen for your

*Self's* thoughts about this person. Each perspective will presence a different paradigm. The journey of life is only about shifting from your *Mind* to your *Self*. It is from your *Self* that you experience what you have come here for—to be your divine nature of love, peace, and oneness with the people in your life.

(To hear an mp3 audio of this exercise, go to www. indiratoday.com/Books/conception4.)

## The Fusion of *Mind, Body,* and *Self*

You are on an eternal journey. The life you are currently living is one of the many times You have chosen to exist in a physical form. It is what You will keep doing over and over again, in order to know yourself as divine, as your True and Highest *Self*. You embody, in your DNA, a resonance that evokes your best and true *Self*, your divine nature. This is who You are, and this is how You experience yourself when you Connect, Listen, Trust, and Act from your *Self*, as distinct from your *Mind*.

Conception is the fusion of a *Mind, Body,* and *Self* as Energy. When you can hold the idea of this fusion as energy, you can begin to claim the distinct dimensions that they bring into the journey you are on. The vibration of the three, as energy, allows you to have a very distinct relationship to each as a whole. The distinction of "fusion" allows you to shift your relationship from the view of the *Mind*—which is, that there is no separation between the *Mind, Body,* and *Self*—to seeing each as having their own distinct design and accessing a new paradigm in the living of your life.

With the *Mind* as a tool for the journey of your *Self*, you have brought forth the intention of conception.

You will be here for what this journey at conception was intended to fulfill and unfold—to be in the experience of your true and highest *Self* in each moment of your life with your *Body* as the vessel that allows for this amazing journey.

When all energies are aligned with your *Self*'s intention, your life flows in an energetic realm where it is naturally and effortlessly aligning with the authentic journey of *Self*. When you are in the Connection to your *Self* as energy, your impact and your presence are beyond the physical plane. Within the energy and vibration of being your *Self*, you impact the world around you, the planet, and the vibration of the universe. You become a divine "knowing" that shifts, not only how those around you vibrate and resonate, but also how the planet and the cosmos resonate. This is the gift of fusion.

## Vibrate, Resonate, Frequency: The Language of Energy

Most people intellectually believe that one day, each of us, will no longer be in our *Body*, but truly "knowing" this is a different thing entirely. In our day-to-day living from our *Mind*, the *Mind* keeps us organized around the physical world as what is real. Thus we are focused on what we need to do and act upon in order to function and survive. So we are now, in this conversation, presencing a new paradigm that we are energy first.

When you meet someone, before you even speak to them, you are struck first by their energy. There is an energy that you are related to about them. When you look at someone, you experience their energy as a presence. They may not say anything, but you can tell a lot about how they are doing from the energy of their *Body*. You can Connect to their energy through their eyes or from their physical presence.

In the current paradigm, you are not organized to relate to energy as a dimension of you. In the new paradigm, "knowing" you are energy is a powerful means to access living in the duality of *Mind* distinct from *Self*. This will give you a tangible relationship to the distinct energies you embody: the *Mind*, the *Body*, and the *Self*.

It is time to allow this new truth to move to the forefront, so that your *Mind* can get organized around this relationship. When you have the energy of your *Self* be who you are, you will have a different experience of life. You will trust and take Actions from your *Self*, that from the *Mind* might be seen as a threat. When you are living from your *Self* as energy, you will be able to Connect to another *Self* as energy. This will give you an experience of people not just as a physical form but as a vibrational force of energy called their *Self*.

Connecting to people this way opens up your relationship with them, not only as a physical form, but as an opportunity for unfolding a journey together, from the energy of your *Selves*. Little do you know that each person in your life opens up and allows for you to fulfill the journey you are on. Connecting to your *Self* with their *Self*, rather than acting from what gets evoked from the *Mind*, leaves both of you present to unfolding your journey together. You come together in your relationship, not from what gets triggered from the *Mind*, but from what the *Selves* are here to accomplish. In being with challenging situations from the *Self's* energy, you can disengage the *Mind's* reactions. This will shift the situation from an upset or an annoyance to an experience of the fundamental energy of *Self* that "all will be fine."

As energy you resonate and vibrate in a particular frequency. The speaking of your *Self* as energy is foreign to the *Mind*. The *Mind* deliberately blocks having a clear relationship with your *Self*. In "knowing" you are energy, you can begin to develop an awareness of how you vibrate and resonate. There is a distinct difference in the vibration and resonance of the frequency of the *Mind* and the frequency of the *Self*.

Imagine that You are a force of energy vibrating and pulsating. Like a moving cloud, You are a mass of energy that is vibrating and resonating as you live your life encountering the different events and circumstances in walking your journey. As you live in your life from the new paradigm of your *Self* as energy, where your Actions are taken from your *Self* distinct from your *Mind*, it activates your "knowing," which alters how you resonate in your life and in the world. This shift in resonance is energetically connected to the "Universal Energy." These energies are real and interconnected. You are aligned, energetically and vibrationally, with the frequency and resonance of the universal consciousness, which is a higher frequency than that of your *Mind* alone. It is here, in claiming your energetic Connection as your only reality, that you experience your *Self* naturally and effortlessly unfolding your life's journey.

Your journey is the releasing of your *Mind's* energy to activate the vibration and resonance of your *Self*. When this happens, you are aligned with a "Universal Energy" that supports the unfolding of your journey from your *Self*. The vibration of your "inner knowing" becomes activated. You now have access to a new dimension of "knowing" that goes beyond the information you learned or experienced. When you are Connecting, Listening, Trusting, and Acting from your *Self*, any area of your life will be aligned with the vibration and resonance of your *Self*. By living your life in the vibration and resonance of your *Self* you are within a new paradigm. You will begin to experience the tranquility and peace that connects you to the divine being that you are.

## Why Energy Is the New Paradigm

Without a clear relationship to the three distinct energies you embody as a new paradigm, you do not have access to your *Self*. Any other possible access will have to come through your *Mind* and, consequently, be skewed and tainted from the energy of the *Mind*. Accessing your *Self* through the *Mind* puts you back into the current paradigm with no distinct relationship between the two.

In the current paradigm you cannot tell the difference between what your *Mind* is saying and what your *Self* is saying. You have to create and presence a new paradigm called "energy" designed around having the vibration and resonance of your *Self* exist as real.

From that vantage the *Mind* can then relate to the new paradigm called energy. Holding your *Self* as energy in the current paradigm, you expand your experience to include the dimension of life that is vaster than the physical reality. By relating to the energy of your *Self* as your reality, the new paradigm becomes your reality and you expand the scope from which you can see what cannot be seen by the *Mind*.

You experience life and people around you from the dimension of your *Self*. You find yourself releasing how the Mind has you experience your thoughts and feelings about situations and people. You become someone who sees the Self of another first. You experience your days as a gift. This occurs, not through the Mind, but simply from "knowing" your Self as who you are.

You find yourself honoring the energy of your Self rather than the Mind's views of what is wrong with you and what there is to be fixed. This is a new state of being, a natural unfolding. It is simply a shift in awareness that allows each moment to be what it was designed to be— an instant of "now" where the linearity of time and the dimension of the Mind are void of their truths. You transcend the physical dimension to hold and be in touch with the "energy" of a situation or a person.

In order for this to occur you must create and embrace the "knowing" that resonates within you—that you are a vibration of energy that transcends the physical realm. This energy is specific. It holds in its vibration all of the experiences you have ever experienced, in your human form, and most importantly, it resonates with all that is your divine nature.

Our essence is divine; it is the innate nature of who we are. We have in our energetic realm all the "knowing" of our divine Self. Presencing energy as a real and tangible dimension of ourselves allows us to Connect to the experience of energy as our divine Self and trust that over the Mind's conversation about what is happening. Some people refer to this as our intuition; however, this still leaves the Mind to define what our intuition is versus living in the "knowing" that we can trust the energy that vibrates as our true Self. We must therefore create a new paradigm where the energy of our Self can exist void of the Mind's view on what is evoked from the energy of our higher Self.

## Energy Is Eternal

From our *Mind*, knowing that energy is eternal is just more knowledge. From our *Self*, "knowing" that energy is eternal brings about a state change in how we vibrate. When we embrace a shift in consciousness by embracing a new truth that shapes and recontextualizes who we are and why we are here, we then align ourselves with the natural flow of the universal unfolding.

We existed before we fused at conception. The existence of our *Self* is not in a physical form and exists as an energetic force of energy that vibrates and resonates in a frequency that emits our highest divine nature. This is who we are. This energy is eternal. That is, it will continue to exist and resonate and vibrate eternally. There is no end or destination, for it is the nature of who we are. Having a *Body* is only for the purpose of living the gift, whereby we get to experience, through our senses, our true *Self*. The eternal nature of energy allows us to activate our true nature, our "inner knowing" as real.

It is in knowing this statement as true and embracing this truth that you gain a powerful access to seeing or holding the *Mind* as a tool for your journey. The "knowing" of energy as eternal allows you to transcend fear and anxiousness and disconnects the illusion of the *Mind* that this physical realm is all that is real. It is through this eternal nature that you can expand your "knowing" of life as a dimension of the journey while *not* being *the* journey. This generates a state change, whereby you can experience your *Self* in the "now" as a way of living. This state change shifts how you resonate, keeping you Connected to your *Self*, as a way of living your life: where your Actions coming from your *Self* are peaceful and void of the *Mind's* illusions of what is real.

Living a new paradigm is bringing forth the energy of your *Mind* and of your *Self* as distinct. The energy of the *Mind* is one of fear, separation, disconnectedness, worry, and getting to a destination. The *Mind* relates to the physical realm as all that is and what is happening in the physical world as all that matters.

The energy of *Self* is one of love, connectedness, oneness, and understanding your divine nature as real and eternal. There is no destination, only the honoring of *Self*.

It is the distinguishing of these two energies that gives you access to a new paradigm. When you can see the *Mind* as a mechanism that is separate from your *Self*, you activate a frequency that presences your true and divine nature. This activation is like tuning into a radio station, one in which you can hear your *Self*. Your *Self* is always transmitting a "knowing" of what honors your highest journey in each moment of "now." When you dwell in this new paradigm of energy as real, you hold the *Mind's* energy and the energy of your *Self* as two separate and distinct energies from which to choose. The choice gives you two separate and distinct realities. You could be someone listening to your *Mind* and acting from your *Mind*, and that will unfold one kind of life. Or you could be someone Listening and Acting from your *Self*, and that would give you another experience of life. No one experience is good or bad; it is simply that one experience is designed around your true *Self* and one is designed around the *Mind*, which is not who you are.

Living from your *Self* as what is real shifts the entire nature of your life. What had You choose to be here becomes what you actually begin to Act on. You are actually having your Actions align with your true essence. It is the seeing of these two energies as separate and distinct that allows you to access and live in a new paradigm.

## Accessing Who You Are as Your *Self*

It is through seeing life through these new lenses that you begin to have a relationship with your *Self*, as who you really are. Without this awareness, the *Mind* creates the determination that your thoughts and whatever is being evoked from the *Mind are* your truth and your reality. Your actions come from what the *Mind* is determining to be real.

By distinguishing the current paradigm as the *Mind* and creating a new paradigm of your *Self*, you can begin to get in touch with your *Self* as real. As you will see in the following chapters, the *Mind* is on a journey to presence the physical realm as the only thing that is real. Your *Self* is here to presence the eternal nature of your journey as real. Therefore, it is hard to access the journey of your *Self* through how the *Mind* sets up your life. The *Mind* simply operates in a way that ensures you never experience your *Self* as who you truly are; it will control your experience in the physical dimension as real, to safeguard your survival. By bringing forth a new paradigm, you can begin to disconnect from the *Mind* and Connect to your *Self*, providing a way to honor the journey You are here to experience.

## Redefining Why You Are Here Provides Access to an Authentic Life

From your *Mind*, your being here is to relate to the physical world around you as what is real. Your *Mind* creates the illusion that it knows what you must do to be successful, live a great life, and become who you are supposed to be. However, since we are not our *Mind*, this leaves us with a relationship to our *Self* that is determined by the *Mind*. This is a disconnect that leaves us in the current paradigm relating to ourselves from our *Mind* not our *Self*. An authentic life is having our Actions come from our *Self*. Many of us do everything we feel is right from the perspective of our *Mind*, yet we find ourselves with unfulfilled relationships, unsatisfying jobs, unhealthy bodies, etc. Life occurs this way because in the current paradigm we have no access to another experience of life.

What if you could unquestionably know that your journey with your partner is eternal and "trust" the eternal nature of your relationship, not just the physical nature? When you activate the dimension of You called your *Self*, in your relationships you naturally bring forth your *Self*. When you can live from your *Self*, all of your life becomes aligned with your journey—the honoring of your *Self* and the *Self* of another. You begin to relate to your situations and circumstances from the journey that You chose to experience. From here, each moment is a new moment for you to activate your highest *Self*. In doing so, you walk the journey of your *Self* as life continues to unfold.

This new paradigm shift redefines why You are here and opens up another context to shape the experience of your life.

## Connecting to *Self* as an Access to Who You Are and Why You Are Here

Connecting to your *Self* is your *only* access to who you are and why you are here. Without Connecting to your *Self*, you are automatically connected to your *Mind*. Almost all of your actions in life come from your *Mind*, as you will see in future chapters. The *Mind* is designed for total and absolute control over the physical realm. But you are not just a physical being. You have a *Body* and a *Mind* so that you can experience your highest *Self*. It is through Connecting to your *Self* and then Listening, Trusting, and Acting from it that you will experience the contextual shift in which your Actions will now be aligned with your *Self* and your purpose. You will live each moment in a "now," in the experience of what there is to know and Act on arising from your *Self*. The following chapters will train you in how to Connect to your *Self* on a regular basis to create this change. This simple shift in awareness and alignment in how you live your life sets the ongoing drive of your *Mind* to be in the background, as you discover the magnificence of your *Self*. This shift is one where you begin to experience the "knowing" that resonates within you, and in this simple shift, you will be at peace. You become someone whose Trust in their *Self* is the journey that is life. It is a moment of redefining a new truth where you are not seeking to find your *Self* in life, but rather you are bringing your *Self* to life. You are at home with your *Self* and you experience life as it was designed to be—a remarkable journey where you get to have the joy of being your *Self*.

Living from your *Self*, distinct from your *Mind* as who you are, is a contextual shift in the design of life. All of life occurs differently. You begin to get organized to experience the difference between your *Self* and your *Mind*. You develop a relationship to your *Self* as who you are and know that having your Actions come from your *Self* will always unfold your true journey and purpose.

You experience a profound relationship to your *Self* as You, as you Connect, Listen, Trust, and Act from your *Self* rather than your *Mind*. Unexplained situations will arise; unimaginable experiences will unfold. You develop a Trusting of your *Self* in the face of the *Mind's* pull and find your*self* willing to step into situations and circum-stances that once felt fearful, wrong, and even danger-ous. You discover yourself Trusting your *Self* in the face of the turmoil around you. The world will continue to ebb and flow with many unpredictable events, but you will be able to live from the context of your *Self* rather than your *Mind* to shape your journey, your purpose, and to fulfill what You presence as your highest and truest *Self*.

## A Paradigm Shift for Humanity

Humanity once lived in a paradigm of knowing that the world was flat, and this "truth" shaped our daily actions and our experience of life. It also created the boundaries and dimensions from which life could be experienced. So too, living from our *Mind* as who we are shapes our daily actions and our experience of life, with boundaries and limits in the dimensions of who we know ourselves to be. This is how we experience ourself in the *Mind's* world when we see no distinction between the *Mind* and our *Self*.

If we can hold our *Mind* as a tool for our journey, we can allow our *Self* to manifest in our daily lives, where our Actions can then come from our highest and truest *Self*. How humanity unfolds—our choices and decisions to create life—will be part of a new paradigm.

That we are energy first is a statement that does not resonate in the current paradigm. Your *Mind* will never have you relate to yourself as energy. From the *Mind*, we can only exist as a physical form. However, as we said earlier, before the fusion of the *Mind*, *Body*, and *Self* at conception, You existed only as energy.

Why is being our highest *Self* a new era for humanity? As we shift from countries operating individually, we will embark on a journey of embracing each other for economic workability. Looking outside ourselves for answers within the current paradigm will only create more of the *Mind* protecting and defending and separating. We will seek answers from what the *Mind* knows it needs to do— survive. The planet will become so small as our access to services, products, and communication becomes more instant and more dependent. What is occurring in one end of the world will dramatically impact another part of the world. We will find ourselves operating in a fear-based energy, or we will shift into a new paradigm of Connecting to our *Self* for what Actions to be in.

When our actions have shifted from our *Mind* to our *Self*, we are embracing the journey of who we are and what our being here is designed to presence and manifest. Our issues and problems will be solved, not by more of the *Mind's* attempt to be logical and survive, but rather by bringing into reality the honoring of each other.

Imagine—no wars!
Imagine—no prisons!
Imagine—no separation in Trusting!

This cannot exist in the current paradigm. We are deeply designed, from the current paradigm of the *Mind*, to come from what the *Mind* has so powerfully operated from: that our survival is the driver of how we set up and organize ourselves.

The new era comes from Trusting our *Self*. Our *Self* is designed around honoring. It lives in the "knowing" that we are safe, we are eternal, and we are here for a journey that allows each of us to Trust the highest expression of who we are. Yes, we will have things we love and enjoy, but we will be resonating in a vibration that has us Connect, Listen, Trust, and Act from our *Self*. We will ignite the divine *Self* within, and when we have embraced this new paradigm, we will bring forth a new era for ourselves. It is a new era for humanity. It is a paradigm shift in how we think and see life and the world and ourselves. In this new era we will create a contextual shift in who we all are and why we are here.

# ⁀ 2 ⁀

# The Current Paradigm:
# The Journey of the Mind

In the current paradigm the *Mind* is what shapes and drives your day-to-day actions. We all live in an automatic truth that who we are is our *Mind* and what it thinks. This truth vibrates as an energy. It is not a function of whether you believe this or not: your cells organize around this truth. The energy that vibrates as the *Mind* is one of fear. It must create the experience of fear for the sake of our survival. This experience creates an energy that has us remove, withdraw, and separate ourselves from perceived threats. From the *Mind*, life itself is an energy of perceived threats that could at any time impact our survival. This is not something you think about consciously; it is as automatic as opening your eyes or breathing. It is simply how the *Mind* operates.

While you may read a lot about your Spirit (or what we have been calling our *Self*) or about the *Mind*, it is only when you relate to both from the perspective of energy that you will experience the difference in how they resonate and vibrate. This is why, in this book, we discuss the *Mind* as the current paradigm. In doing so, we can now distinguish the *Mind* for its role so that we can see how it works as well as its design and contribution to living our lives. It is only then that we can see past it to reveal another aspect of ourself called our *Self*.

The *Mind's* relationship to the journey of life is from the viewpoint that life is only about what exists in the physical realm. The *Mind* receives images and information from all of our five senses, and what is experienced by the *Mind* is our reality. This information is related to us as real and is used anytime the *Mind* is triggered by a situation. From the *Mind* life is *only* about what the *Mind* thinks is appropriate action. There is no other reality. Life is organized around what we are doing, feeling, wanting, and should be having while we are here in the physical realm.

## What Truths the *Mind* Embodies

In the energy of the how the *Mind* vibrates and resonates, you naturally exist within the following truths:

- The thoughts you are hearing *are* who you are.

- The physical realm is the *only* reality that exists.

- What it sees and hears is real.

- Everything must be recognized and dealt with to survive.

- Dying is never a reality until the moment it happens.

- Everything and everyone are expendable if your survival is threatened.

As a vibration and resonance, these truths are housed at the cellular level. As such, there is no thinking or viewpoint about what is spoken as these truths. It simply is a dimension of the energies that you embody when you live from the current paradigm. It is the energy in which the Mind resonates and vibrates, shaping how you think and view situations, people, circumstances, and life itself. It is an experience that is embodied in your DNA as your truth. It shapes what you experience as your reality.

The vibration of the Mind is the energy of fear, separation, survival, control, worry, and concern. We all live in this reality as naturally as a fish swims in water. It is our existence from our Mind. It becomes the context for why we are here and where our actions come from. The Mind shares the reality that our being here is about: the things we own, what we are doing, what we need to have, and what we need to know. Most of our time is spent on what the Mind perceives to be what makes us happy, what is best for us, what we should look like, what we need to be happy, what is important to us in our life, the truths that are shaped by our culture, our beliefs, and all that our Mind has concluded is necessary and important to live a good life. Our daily routines include what the Mind wants based on our survival. Whoever gets there first, wins. Am I keeping up with the Joneses? Am I getting my piece of the pie?

The impact of this is that we experience almost no joy in being in the moment. We are disconnected from the joy of our Self. We find ourselves on a journey of looking for what we need to be doing, having, or being in each moment. This is all coming from what the Mind is now determining is the next appropriate action to fulfill what it thinks is next for us.

Take a piece of paper. Look out in front of you and write down *every* thought you have for the next five minutes about whatever comes to *Mind*. This is not a reporting of what you see; it is about what gets triggered from your *Mind* as you look out. After the five minutes are up, go back and read what you have put down. Notice the concerns and worries.

## How Knowing You Are Not Your *Mind* Shifts How You Resonate and Vibrate

Every moment you bring forth an awareness that you are not your *Mind* and you can observe it, you immediately shift how you vibrate and resonate. The act of thinking— I am not my *Mind*—is a shift from the energy of the *Mind* as the only reality. You have just activated a new truth: that there is a You separate from the *Mind*. This engenders a vibrational shift on the cellular level. You immediately disconnect from the truths that the *Mind's* energy is organized around and begin to activate your cells and your DNA to organize around another dimension of your being called your *Self*.

The *Mind's* energy will always resonate the strongest and loudest, dominating your thoughts. Nevertheless, choosing your *Self*, distinct from your *Mind*, shifts you into a new paradigm. This alters how you vibrate and sets up a different experience of your life. It allows you to activate the vibration and resonance of your *Self* as real. This *only* occurs when you choose to relate to the *Mind* as *not* who you are.

The *Mind* is designed to support you in living life as a human being. Its design is to ensure your survival, and it always operates with that purpose. The mechanism of the *Mind* is not designed to fulfill and unfold your journey as a spiritual being on a spiritual journey. This clear distinction is where you begin when you engage in understanding the mechanism of the Mind. By knowing the mechanics of the Mind, you can begin to relate to the Mind for its journey, as a tool, in living from your Self as a way of life.

The mechanism of the Mind is to always have absolute control. This statement is one to presence, so take a moment to pause and bring forth the awareness of this. Think about it: if our Mind's mechanism is out for absolute control, then where does that leave us in having any relationship to our Self?

Everything that exists in the current paradigm is controlled by your Mind, including how you are Connected to your Self. Therefore you have to create a new paradigm from which to access and live from your Self.

It is the nature of the Mind to ensure that whatever is occurring will eventually be dealt with by what your Mind has stored about that situation. How you should feel, what you should think, what emotions apply to the situation, etc.—all of what is occurring is shaped by how the Mind relates to what has occurred. From the Mind, absolute control is necessary for survival and to protect you from all perceived danger. Danger signals triggered from the Mind are not only expressing just what is occurring in reality, they are also relating to what is stored in the Mind's vibration that presences what should be feared. Often we find ourselves taking actions that may come from the fear of a situation, when in reality there is no actual danger from or fear of the person, situation, or circumstance occurring in that moment. The depth of the control of the Mind is absolute, it is vast, and it will always operate in this mechanical way. It is in knowing this that you can allow the *Mind* to operate as it is designed. When you are struggling with the need to control a situation, you can notice it and let it go, knowing that this is not you, it is the *Mind*. You don't have to act on what the *Mind* is saying in that moment. You can begin to engage in a new view and a new relationship to your *Mind* to understand how it operates and what the *Mind's* mechanism is designed to evoke in your life.

It is common knowledge that we have a *Mind*. We universally agree that we have a *Mind*, even though we have never seen our *Mind*. We relate to and embrace the *Mind* as a normal part of us. Most of us also know we have a *Self*. However, knowing this does not make the *Self* as immediately available to us as our *Mind* is. Instead, this understanding lives in the background of the *Mind* as mere information. We live our lives unaware that we have a choice to either Listen to our *Self* or our *Mind*. We simply live from our *Mind* talking to us all day and all night, and we listen to our *Mind* like it is who we are. In the current paradigm there is no distinction of the *Mind* and *Self* as a possible choice for getting the answers for living a more fulfilled life.

### Nigel, Project Manager

I relate to the *Mind* in different ways at different times. There are times when I'm completely within the *Mind* and it's in total control, and there are times within the experience of Connecting to my *Self* that I'm able to step back and observe the *Mind* from the outside, and know that "Hey, there's all this stuff that's happening in there," but it's not the core of who I am. My *Mind* is always racing, but I've been able to kind of step back and disconnect and observe. I've gone from being completely pulled into everything the *Mind* is saying about life experiences to, almost on a constant basis, having an underlying awareness that this is not true, this is the *Mind*. For example, before I would go into a meeting with my project team at work, and my *Mind* would be racing, and it would be all about, "let me figure this out, let me figure this out, let me figure this out," and "how do I get us going in this particular direction?" or "let me get this other person to see this idea through the same lens I see it." Now I get into a meeting with the project team, and it's just completely different. It's more about letting things unfold throughout the meeting, letting everyone offer their own perspective, and I Trust that even if something is different than how I would deal with it, it's still going to be okay. And I've seen that being reinforced in the way the team has responded to me and how everyone has become much more empowered and engaged. That's actually created phenomenal results with different teams I've been interacting with in the business, and I've just seen a completely different level of thinking and interacting going on with the people on the team through no particular actions of my own with them. It's become less about allowing my *Mind* to drive things in a particular direction and more about just allowing people to contribute their own ideas. That, for me, is very impactful.

## Embracing the *Mind* as a Necessary Part of Your Journey

The *Mind* is a part of who you are. It is a powerful and necessary dimension of your life as a human being. Relating to the *Mind* as a tool for your journey allows you to honor the *Mind* for the role it is truly designed to play in how you live your life.

Your *Mind* is central to your existence on the physical plane. It records each second of your experiences and stores all that information to be reapplied in every situation. As part of its mechanism you will find yourself in its absolute control over everything you do. It must operate and be honored for what it provides in how you live your life and exist in the physical realm. It protects you from danger by registering any and all circumstances that may pose a threat.

The truth is you need your *Mind* to connect you to your five senses, allowing you to function in a physical form. It lets you see and operate powerfully in the physical realm. You cannot exist on the physical plane without a *Mind*. It is the part of you committed to your survival. It is the part of you that drives your life from the moment you wake up to the moment you go to bed. What you do, how you do it, why you do it, and when you do it are all designed and driven by the *Mind*. You need to eat, clothe yourself, and operate and function in different climates and environments. Your knowing how to react or retreat, depending on the situation, as well as how to operate and function with the tools you need to exist in the world, is all driven by the *Mind*.

The *Mind* is what speaks and drives all of what you instinctively know to do and when and how to do it. You learn and grow and discover how to function in the world through your *Mind*. Without your *Mind*, you cannot function in life.

The *Mind* is also a powerful tool for the journey of your *Self* when it is related to in its intended role. Your

*Self* is an energy, a vibration that is not physical. It exists as an energy, a vibration that encompasses all the "knowing" of your true and divine *Self*. It is only when the *Mind* embraces this *Self* as real that you can exist and operate as your *Self*. When you can Connect, Listen, Trust, and Act from your *Self*, the *Mind* becomes a tool for the journey of your *Self*. This shifts the role the *Mind* plays to include a relationship to your *Self* as real.

You cannot exist in a new paradigm without the *Mind* as a tool for the journey your *Self* is here to unfold and manifest. The *Mind* is the core of your connection to the physical plane. Using it as a tool for the journey of your *Self* will bring a new paradigm into play in your life.

## The Patterns of the *Mind*

The *Mind*, like our *Self*, is an eternal energy. Our *Mind* is included as part of the fusion at conception, for it is a necessary dimension of our eternal journey. As was mentioned before, we cannot exist in the physical realm without a *Mind*. It houses in its vibration all of what we have experienced, everything that has ever evoked fear, and all the situations and events that we have experienced as threatening to our existence. This has nothing to do with the situations, but rather with whatever and whenever the *Mind* is triggered by a perceived threat or fear of a situation.

Remember: the *Mind* is not You, but it has a role that operates as if it were You. The *Mind* has a world it is holding, seeing, watching, and operating in, and as we take actions based on what the *Mind* thinks and feels, it logs and tracks all actions as true. The situations you experience while in a physical form become a part of your journey that is eternal. These are stored at a DNA level.

When you choose to enter a physical form again, the *Mind* once more becomes a part of the journey. Each person's *Mind* is distinctly designed to ensure surviving this journey. Each time the *Self* fuses with a *Body* and a *Mind*, the *Mind* is already resonating with previous experiences on how to relate to and think in situations, such that we protect ourselves from perceived fears and dangers. However, from the *Mind's* perspective we are not dealing with perceived threats, but with real dangers. If you had a situation in another life where you were threatened, the *Mind* logs the experience for your next life. In your current life, you will find yourself making choices about situations that are based in a different lifetime. The *Mind* is always shaping our experiences from past lives that the *Mind* has survived.

What we do or don't do, how we feel or relate to things that are happening around us, the choices and actions we take or don't take in our life—these are all shaped from these fears or impressions that the *Mind* has tagged as good, bad, dangerous, or fearful. The *Mind* is designed to safeguard your survival and will do anything to maintain that truth.

Without bringing forth as an awareness that you are not your *Mind*, you are limited by what your *Mind* is here to control and survive. You live, by default, from what the *Mind* is saying and how it is operating, and you don't experience what you are here to manifest and fulfill. The *Mind* will always be the driver of your life—it is strong, absolute, and takes total control energetically when possible.

As you are beginning to see, the *Mind* is here for one journey, and it is optimized for the role it is here to play.

Given the design of the *Mind*, living your life from your *Mind* as who you are will never lead to experiencing and living the life you chose to experience when your *Self* chose to enter a *Body*.

The *Mind* is designed to only relate to your physical realm as what is real. It is designed to have you take in what is occurring in the physical world around you and tag what is happening based on the *Mind's* past about how you should feel. Consequently, your actions are aligned with what the *Mind* has determined you should feel and think about life, situations, who you are, and what your being here is about. This is very important to note. As more and more information is available to us effortlessly through the various forms of media and communication technologies—the *Mind* is becoming more and more enmeshed in what it is seeing, hearing, and reading as real. Remember the *Mind* is a mechanism, like a computer. It is all mechanics and logic, and it stores all information and feelings about what is occurring.

The *Mind* relates to what is occurring around us as real and we begin to have more of our *Mind* feed us what we should do, who we should be, what things we need to be and do or have; it is *all* coming from what the Mind has taken in and is now feeding into our consciousness as what is real. Without the distinction, "we are not our *Mind*," we end up living a very mindful life. We have our days filled with a life lived totally from our *Mind*, and that life is void of anything to do with our *Self* and why we chose to be here. We take our last breath in the knowing that we never activated or honored our true *Self*.

## Why It Matters to Know the Design of Your *Mind*

Given the intricate nature of the *Mind* and its dominant control in how it exists in the *Mind-Body-Self* connection, it is critical and necessary that you develop a relationship to the design of the *Mind*. It is only when you have a deep knowing and appreciation for the role the *Mind* plays in your life in the physical world that you can have a powerful relationship to your *Self* as real. You will never get rid of the *Mind*, remove the *Mind*, or not have a *Mind*. Your *Mind* is as necessary and important as your *Self* is in the journey. It is choosing to relate to your *Mind* as not who you are, and knowing the difference between your *Mind* and your *Self*, that allows you to have access to your *Self* as a real and tangible energy.

Knowing the design of your *Mind* allows you to see how your *Mind* is operating and functioning as well as the ways it has designed itself as an eternal energy, such that you can begin to see the *Mind* as it plays out in your life. Knowing the design of your *Mind* allows you to see the *Mind* as it is carrying out its role. When you can see the *Mind* at work, you can recognize it as merely the *Mind*, and you can begin to relate to it as *not* you. This gives you the choice to act either from the *Mind* or from the *Self*. When this distinction is not recognized, then the *Mind* simply runs your life.

The *Mind* is designed to ensure your protection from any and all perceived dangers or threats. Everyone is a threat. Our *Self* is a threat. That is the nature and energy of the *Mind's* vibration. Given this is the vibration that resonates as the *Mind*, the energy of love cannot exist in this same frequency. Do you wonder why relationships are such a strong energy in our lives as human beings?

It is where we play out the duality of *Mind* and *Self* most powerfully. It is only in our being with others that we ignite the energy of *Mind* and *Self* as an experience. As such, relationships become the place where the energy of the *Mind* is dominant, for the *Mind* houses the patterns designed to have us experience ourselves as separate and alone.

Your journey, from the view of the *Self*, is to presence the energy of love. The *Mind* is designed and vibrates to ensure love does not resonate, for it is a threat to the *Mind's* energy of protecting you from perceived dangers. In the design, any connection to what could open you up to being totally vulnerable is a threat. Sometimes we think that outside circumstances are the reasons why our relationships don't work or don't embody the experience of deep joy and fulfillment. This includes our own relationship to loving our selves.

In the patterns of the *Mind*, there are thousands of experiences: the *Mind* has stored information on situations and events where something occurred and tagged many as unsafe or dangerous to prevent them from occurring again. It could be as simple as someone saying something to you that makes you feel like you are not enough (beautiful enough, smart enough, lovable enough). Something happens, and the *Mind* reacts to it immediately. This is always occurring. It is the nature of the machinery, the mechanism of the design of the *Mind*. This experience the *Mind* has tagged triggers thoughts that might include: they don't like me, I am not beautiful, I don't fit in, etc. For human beings, fitting in is part of surviving. So when these thoughts get triggered, the *Mind* will react strongly. The *Mind* has a huge history of being hurt by others, so being vulnerable is also a threat to our survival. These thoughts are registered as a truth and are now embodied in your DNA as real. As you will see in the next chapter, your *Self* evokes a totally different experience and is designed to only presence love and honoring of *Self* and the highest *Self* in each other.

## Nicole, Stay-at-Home Mom, Custom Baking

I've gotten pretty good at knowing when my *Mind* is taking over a situation. My *Mind's* energy is always like, "What are you talking about? You don't know what you're talking about, that's stupid!" It's always belittling; it's always negative. It says things like, "you can't do that." It doesn't believe in me, it holds me back, it's all those things. But when I Listen to my *Self*, it's always a little quiet, it's sure of itself, it's good, it never has too much detail. It's always very profound and I can understand it because it's from my *Self*, whereas the *Mind's* energy is always beating me up and telling me I can never get it right, and I'm no good, and "who do I think I am?" So anything that comes from that space, I know is coming from my *Mind*. And that's how I can tell the difference.

## The Relationship of the *Mind* and *Self*

Given the nature, vibration, and resonance of the *Mind's* role to allow you to function on the physical plane, there is no relationship to your *Self* as real. The *Mind* is like a car going on track A with no interest in giving access to a track B, the track of your *Self*. There is no reason to even know there is a track B, given the *Mind*. It is strong, powerful, and has absolute control of our experience of life. When you have had situations where you did not act from your *Mind*, but Trusted your intuitive *Self*, they become times you can remember. Trusting your intuitive *Self* does not occur as a regular or ordinary way to be, but rather feels extraordinary and not reproducible. We read of and listen to people who have taken actions not given by the ordinary way the *Mind* works, and we are inspired, moved, or feel that these are different, good, better, or right. Most people don't have this happen on a regular basis because the *Mind* dismisses it as luck or good fortune.

It is simply that the *Mind* is a dominant energy and will always reclaim the journey it is here to ensure—our survival. Our relationship to what the *Mind* says and does determines what we will do.

A human being can go through the most horrific experience and still live life. We will always rise up to do what we need to do—eat, clothe ourself, find shelter, find a way to get the money to buy the necessities. We are designed around the basic and necessary actions we need to take to continue to live. This is the role of the *Mind*.

## "Karmic Energies"—How the *Mind* Is Designed to Use Up Your Time in Life

"Karmic energies" are energies from your past that get triggered by some person or situation in life. They are designed to use up your time in life and never give you access to your *Self*. A "karmic energy" is arising whenever you get upset, annoyed, concerned, or worried.

"Karmic energies" are energies that resonate in the *Mind* as a truth about you, others, and situations. These energies are experienced, again, as real in this lifetime when you feel threatened or sense a perceived danger. They are simply reconfirming the truths your *Mind* came into life with.

The "karmic energies" are designed to keep you from being in a "now" and leave you in some experience from the *Mind*, typically feeling upset, annoyance, concern, or worry that appears to be real. "Karmic energies" are formulated from "vows" (decisions) the *Mind* makes about situations and life. The situations the *Mind* perceives as similar will create the same feelings that were experienced when the "karmic energy" originated. For *most* of your life, the *Mind* is playing out these energies and making the original "vows" (decisions) real *again* in your life. It is, in part, how the *Mind* is designed. It has to have these "vows" be real to have the world look a particular way.

Without having a relationship to the term of art "karmic energies," as it is spoken here, we spend most of our life in one of these "karmic energies" and never know our true *Self*. These energies vibrate at a cellular level as who you are and shape your actions.

If you have as a "vow" (decision) "I will never trust again," You will find yourself being cautious and leery of people you don't know or who look a particular way. Being in a personal relationship will leave you always wondering what your partner is doing. If they are gone longer than you think they should be, your *Mind* starts to create illusionary scenarios. Then you wonder why your relationships are not nurturing, satisfying, and loving.

All of our actions, when taken from our *Mind*, are shaped by the "karmic energies" embodied in the patterns of our *Mind*: these patterns are housed in a "vow" that was spoken when we experienced a significant moment in time, in a human form. The "vows" create a truth about how life is for us, such that our *Mind* aligns our actions with ensuring these perceived dangerous situations occur again to survive.

As we live our lives, these "vows" are shaping through our *Mind* what we think and how we act in situations and circumstances. It is where the *Mind* goes to seek out how we are to act in our daily life. For example, emotional eating is a trigger that houses some "karmic energy" or "vow" about yourself or life.

The critical part here is the logic of the *Mind*. It is designed to make the connection to the "vow" and then have our actions correlate to the "vow." It is why we may find ourselves taking actions that make perfect sense, but still leave us feeling empty or knowing that it does not fulfill who we are.

In life the *Mind* is mostly acting within a "karmic energy." The mirage here is that what occurs from the *Mind* is never what occurred from our *Self*. The *Mind* keeps replaying the same *old* "karmic energies."

The cycle of a "karmic energy" is that a situation or a person evokes an energy within you that triggers an energy from your *Mind*; you and they start to play out a patterned role that will end at some point in time (an hour, a day, a week, or longer) and leave you in a decision ("vow") about you, them, and life that is a confirmation of the original "vow." It then resets itself to play again. All of the people in your life, you have "set up" to have your "karmic energies" keep playing out, using up all your time.

- Look at the last time you got upset, annoyed, concerned, or worried.

- Write down the whole story your Mind told you about you, them, and the situation.

- Write down or underline the "decisions" you can see the Mind made about people, you, the situation, and life. These are just confirming an original "vow."

- By writing down these "vows," you will have access to them when the same "karmic energy" comes up again, and you can bring an awareness to the situation that it is evoking a "karmic energy." You can then start to transcend it by Connecting.

Rather than using up your life being consumed by these energies, you can shift and transcend them by Connecting to what there is to know from your *Self* about the situation, the person, and your journey. This is new paradigm, a new reality. Imagine your life having transcended the "karmic energies," allowing you to have a more natural and effortless journey in Trusting your *Self*.

## How Identifying "Karmic Energies" Shifts You into a New Vibration of Energy

When you can identify your "karmic energies," you can shift out of the dominant Mind's energies to accessing your *Self*. You have released a truth that is being played out by the Mind as your reality. These energies are very powerful and impact you and the people in your life. They shape your actions. While you may have an understanding of the situation, these energies are at play and have more of an impact than your intellectual understanding of what is happening. Imagine that the choice you made to be here included transcending the "karmic energies" embodied in your Mind as truths. These energies resonate in your DNA as real. There is no distinction between real and not real when a "karmic energy" is experienced. It occurs for your *Mind* as what is real. Remember that "karmic energies" are from your past, though your *Mind* makes it seem like your responses are caused by the situation that is happening now. Personal relationships are a great place to see this. Did you ever wonder why someone you're in a personal relationship with now starts to behave like the last person you were with?

To start to shift this, you need to bring an awareness forth that this is not you—that these are energies and patterns of the *Mind* playing out within your life. Your vibration will then begin to shift to another frequency and resonance. In this shift in vibration, you align yourself with the frequency of your highest *Self*. You embody the You of your true *Self*, and life naturally manifests what there is for you to know. You begin to experience your *Self* as who you are; you begin to activate your "inner knowing" as You.

The design and role of the *Mind* is to ensure you experience karmic energies as real. Given the *Mind's* role and design, to disengage the wiring that holds the *Mind's* role in place requires creating the awareness that any upset, annoyance, concern, or worry has disconnected you from the "now" of your life. In these moments, take a deep breath and bring awareness to the fact that what is occurring for you has pulled you into a past. Yes, the other person in the situation is saying and doing what they are doing, *but* it does not mean what the *Mind* is making it mean. The *Mind* is designed to have "karmic energies" be who we are. These "karmic energies" are set up to replay themselves in our lives, ensuring we are always out to protect ourselves from perceived fears about situations that are occurring in our life.

For the *Mind*, "karmic energies" *are* real. This tells you a lot about the *Mind's* design and how it is set up to perpetuate realities that no longer exist in your life now. Creating this awareness allows you to disengage the energies of the *Mind* that keep in existence a reality that is not real. This illusion keeps you disconnected from your true *Self* and stops you from living in the "now."

## Including the *Mind* in Life

Having said all that, your *Mind* is a dimension of you that you want to honor and embrace. It is not about not having a *Mind* or not wanting a *Mind*. You have a *Mind*, like you have a *Body* and a *Self*. If you don't have a *Body*, you are not alive. If you don't have a *Self*, you are not alive. If you don't have a *Mind*, you are not alive. The *Mind* is what allows you to function within your *Body*. It is through the *Mind* that you process your thoughts, allowing you to function through your five senses. You want to create a relationship to your *Mind* for what it is—its role and its function.

This relationship, once established, allows you to have access to your *Self* as real. Understanding how your *Mind* functions and how your specific *Mind* is designed— as well as the "karmic energies" and patterns of the *Mind*—allows more access to your *Self*. The more you bring language to the energy of the *Mind* and identify the energies of your *Mind*, the less it will operate in the illusion that it is who you are. You will stop letting your *Mind's* thoughts be what you have to act on. You can make a choice to see the *Mind* as separate from who you are by knowing that your *Self* is who you are and recognizing that you have a *Mind*. It is only by including the *Mind* that you get access to the depth and breadth of your *Self* and the life it came here to experience in this lifetime by having your actions come from your *Self*.

## Why It Matters That You Live from a New Truth That You Are Not Your *Mind*

Given what we are naturally engaged in when we are living from our *Mind* as our only reality, it matters to engage in a new truth that you are not your *Mind*. When you can begin to live in this truth, you can shift your awareness to another dimension of your *Self*. You can engage the dimension of you that is here for a life void of fear, concern, worry, and separation as a natural way of life. It is important to notice when you are not in the awareness that you are not your *Mind*. From your *Mind* you are unable to allow your *Self* to exist as who you are. In the *Mind*'s absolute control and dominant energy as your only reality, you are lost to the "knowing" of your *Self*—for it is the *Mind* that is processing and unfolding life—even when you are consciously here for a higher purpose.

It is *only* when you begin to live from a new truth—that you are *not* your *Mind*—that you can embrace a new paradigm where you can begin to Trust and Act from your *Self*. It is very difficult to access your *Self* from the current paradigm of the *Mind*; the *Mind*'s design will not allow its existence.

## ⪻ 3 ⪼

# The New Paradigm:
# The Journey of *Self*

In the introduction I described the first time I discovered the Connection to my *Self*. I recall completely Connecting to this place that was inside of me. The vibration of it was very real. I experienced this force that felt as solid as being able to touch something in the physical world. It was a feeling at first, and as I related to it as being as real as the physical world around me, language arose. I actually heard this energy or force, like it was life. The more I related to it as real, the more the vibration filled a space inside me that I could never fill before. Questions like "who am I?" and "why am I here?" disappeared, and I became Connected to all of life. The disconnection I had felt all my life disappeared. In this experience, which occurred in a single moment, there was this rejoicing, this inner dancing, and this deep, deep joy of feeling this "me" at the depth that it was. It was like a deep, deep Connection that was now forever Connected. And then I could hear my *Self* speaking to me and saying, "I am You." The more often I Connected, the easier it became to hear it. It became a consciousness that never went away, and the flow of it sounded like this: "I am here. I am You. I am in every fiber of your being. I am your *Self*." And the vibrational energy that I got from this force was love and joy and a sense that it is there for everything and anything I need. It vibrated as, "Come here, to this vibration that is You, called *Self*, and Connect, Listen, Trust, and Act, and know that when you do that, you will naturally unfold who you are and why you are here. From this place you will know that 'all will be well,' and 'all will be as it should be.'" The knowing of this statement as true resonated and permeated each cell and presenced a "knowing" that transcended all of my *Mind's* beliefs about me and life around me.

So I began to do what I heard. And from that moment, that truth became my truth—it became the truth of who I am.

When you begin to relate to energy as another dimension of You, you begin to experience how you vibrate and resonate. This occurs as you develop Listening to tell the difference between the energy of how the *Mind* resonates and how your *Self* resonates. We saw in the last chapter that the *Mind's* vibration is loud, urgent, commanding, and demanding; it's about control and survival, and it's always reacting to what's going on around you. It is like a little child who wants something. Have you ever noticed that when your *Mind* is triggered by something that has upset you, whether it is something your wife, husband, or partner said or a project at work that isn't going the way you wanted it to, the *Mind* is like a dog with a bone. It won't let it go; you think about it constantly, even when you are doing other things. It is like a bell clanging, a constant and annoying vibration saying, "Something is wrong here," as you try to go on about your day. Connecting to your *Self* can quiet the *Mind* and certainly give you direction about how to handle the situation in a way that will have everything turn out in alignment with your journey. Connecting is never about excluding the *Mind*; it is always going to be there. Instead, it is about harmonizing the vibrations of *Mind* and *Self*—together.

When the *Mind* is being loud and overactive, here is a tool to help you quiet it:

1. Stop, close your eyes, and take a deep breath.

2. As you breathe in deeply, imagine surrounding yourself in light. Breathe in the light, and as you exhale, imagine all the worries of the *Mind* floating away like little bubbles in the wind. Let go of all of the worry and concern and fear.

3. Presence the knowing that your *Mind* is not You. Continue to release its control as you bring forth the "knowing" of your *Self* as You.

4. Hold the energy of your *Self* as real. Let that vibration become real for you.

5. Allow yourself to be in the vibration of your *Self* knowing that "all is well."

(To hear an mp3 audio of this exercise, go to www. indiratoday.com/Books/newparadigm.)

The *Self* sounds very different from the *Mind*. The resonance of your *Self* is *always* one of deep love, compassion, and honor. It is an experience of being Connected to everything in a resonance of oneness with others and even with the universe itself. This is the truth of who you are, and when you are Acting from this energy, you are within the experience of your true *Self*. The *Self's* vibration is softer than the *Mind*, that is why in the beginning you will need to set up a specific practice of Connecting in which you learn how to quiet the *Mind* and Listen for your *Self*. The *Self's* vibration is soft and assuring, never urgent.

You are embarking on a shift in your experience of *who you are*. If your Actions are coming from love, compassion, honor, and being Connected to everyone as your *Self*, you are then in touch with your truest and highest *Self*.

## How Your *Self* Relates to the Journey of Life

Your *Self* relates to the journey of life as a gift to experience the nature of *Self*. The nature of *Self* is to honor. To honor is to have an open heart. The journey of life, as you saw from the chapter on the current paradigm, is destined from the *Mind* to be an experience of fear and separation and survival. The journey of your *Self* is to be a journey of peace and joy and the deep, profound gift that life offers—the physical opportunity to experience being fearless, connected to others, and to bring that to your moment-by-moment exploration on the physical plane in this lifetime.

Your *Self* relates to the journey of life as a journey experienced in each moment of "now," knowing that You are eternal and that the *Body* is a vessel to be honored, for it allows you to be in the journey. Your *Self* relates to the journey of life by bringing your *Self* to life, which is different from going to life to find your *Self*.

While you will be doing all of what you need to be doing from the current paradigm, this is not what the purpose of your life is about. Many people express feeling as if they have not yet found their purpose in life or not feeling fulfilled in what they are doing or what their life is about. What is missing is that they have not yet Connected with their *Self* to unfold the journey they were born into this lifetime for. The journey of life from your *Self* is to use the current paradigm as the pathway to express your highest *Self*. It lets you have a new view from which to see life, a new perspective from which to hear life, and new ways of thinking where you can integrate your *Self* and your *Mind*. The *Mind* can now be a tool for the journey your *Self* is here to express and manifest, each day, each moment for as long as you are in your physical form.

## The Truths That Embody the Vibration and Resonance of Your *Self*

How you resonate and vibrate as *Self* presences a new paradigm. It is a paradigm that shapes a new perspective for humanity. This new paradigm redefines why you are here and what your life is about. You've already seen the truths the *Mind* resonates with. In the resonance and vibration of this new paradigm, there are new truths:

- You are eternal, a spiritual being on a spiritual journey.

- You are energy and everything is energy, each having its own vibration.

- You are not your *Mind*. You have a *Mind*, and the *Mind* can be in service to your *Self*'s journey.

- The world, the physical dimension of life, is there to evoke experiences that are designed to open up more access to your *Self* as you transcend the *Mind*'s energy.

- Each of us chose to come here from our *Self*, and inherent in each of us is a higher *Self*.

Let's take a deeper look at these truths:

You are eternal, a spiritual being on a spiritual journey. In this energy you can hold, at any time of your life, a new context that you are not limited to the physical plane. This "knowing" brings forth a new frequency with which you may activate energies within you that allow you to transcend the physical realm of life as your only paradigm.

You are energy and everything is energy, each having its own vibration. When you can view and relate to every situation as your journey, you activate the energy of your *Self* and Connect to what is there for you to know about what is happening. This puts you within your journey, bringing your *Self* to life, and has the people, situations, and events be what you have "set up" to experience—to transcend some dimension of the *Mind* to know your true *Self*.

You are not your *Mind*. You have a *Mind*, and the *Mind* can be in service of your journey. This new truth shapes life very differently. When you can access and activate this truth, in a moment, in any moment, you can release your *Mind's* thoughts and embrace what your *Self* is presencing. Your *Self* will always presence your true, highest expression of the divine nature of who you are.

Each situation you experience is directly related to your journey and what there is for you to discover about your *Self*. The world, the physical dimension of life, is there to evoke experiences that are designed to open up more access to your *Self*.

The journey of life is the moment-by-moment transcending of the *Mind* to Connect, Listen, Trust, and Act from your *Self*. In this way, you unfold the spiritual journey your *Self* is on—You are a spiritual being on a spiritual journey.

Fusion is the moment of choosing to have a *Body* where your *Mind* and your *Self* can play out the journey. When You leave, there is nothing about the physical plane that you take with you . . . not even your *Body*. From the new paradigm there is a contextual shift in what is actually occurring in life as the journey. The journey you are on is to experience your *Self* as real, and given what you have seen about how the *Mind* is designed, you are, in each moment, transcending the *Mind* to honor your *Self*. It is here that you begin to shift the "karmic energies" of the *Mind* to naturally and effortlessly have your Actions come from *Self*.

Each of us chose to come here from our *Self*, and inherent in each of us is a higher *Self*—a divine presence that is resonating. When we begin to live from the new paradigm as our *Self*, we will shift the shape of humanity. When we live from our *Self* as real, we honor the *Self* of each person as an energy of higher vibration—their true *Self*. This has us relate to each other in a different way than simply human to human. It will be a very different world when we are relating to each other from this higher vibration of *Self*—honoring the *Self* in each person we meet.

## The Energetic Vibration of Your *Self* and Its Impact on How You Relate to Life

The energy of your *Self* is a vibration that activates that dimension of you that is your eternal divine *Self*. Imagine if we were all living from that part of us, as a way of life. You can begin to see that there is another paradigm that exists simultaneously, as much as we have a paradigm that is designed from our *Mind*. When you choose to honor the vibration of your *Self* as who you are and what is real, you bring to life the highest expression of your *Self*. Clearly this is a paradigm shift for humanity.

Imagine how things will be when rather than having our actions come from our own individual survival nature of the "me" energy, that is the energy of the *Mind*, they arise from one in which we can Trust that we will be taken care of, and we can begin to see life from a higher plane. We can exist within a larger conversation about what and where our Actions will come from, shifting our paradigm to making an impact, at any moment, by simply choosing to Act from *Self*.

We will begin to see life not from limitations, but rather from a moment-by-moment choice to Trust and Act from our *Self*. This means that we are shifting the context off of making money or having money as our primary focus, and instead are looking to experience the life we are here to live from *Self*.

When we can activate our *Self* as an energy from which we begin to Connect, Listen, Trust, and Act, we bring forth what we came here to be for our *Self* and each other. We become the solution to the problems we are having and facing as individuals, as a society, as a nation, and as a global community. We find ourselves transcending our fears and developing a Trusting of our *Self* that allows the *Mind* to get very quiet; we begin to hear the communication from our *Self* as a new paradigm. Our Actions begin to shape what we are bringing to the world around us, as we live in a duality that allows us to honor our *Self*, while transcending our *Mind*, to harmonize the two.

## Jennifer, Hair Salon Owner

There have been several times when I've Connected and the message I got from *Self* was so different from what my *Mind* would normally have me say and do, so I knew it didn't come from my *Mind*. For example, I had a falling out with my sister-in-law. There was a situation, and she and I got into it about it. It was a big thing in my family, and we pretty much stopped talking. I was Connecting one day, and I wasn't even Connecting about her, but I got from my *Self* that she and I should talk. My first reaction was like, "Yeah, right, I'm not even going to go there; that's not going to happen." But it came up for me several times when I was Connecting over that weekend. It just kept resonating that she and I needed to talk. So I finally took Action on it and sent her an email saying, "Look, I want to talk. You're my family, you're my brother's wife, I don't want there to be any animosity between us." And so we went to dinner and had probably a two-hour conversation, and we resolved every issue that was there for both of us. Out of that, I now have a relationship with my sister-in-law, which makes me feel so much better because I adore her children and my niece is the love of my life. So it just made my life and, hopefully, my brother's life so much easier. So that was something that was really powerful, because usually from my *Mind*, I would not go there at all. It would have said, "Look, this is just how it is." But I Connected and then I Trusted and Acted from what I got and that was the result, and I'm really glad I did. I Connect around any situation that I feel is significant in my life.

## How "Knowing" You Are Your *Self* Shifts the Frequency in Which You Resonate and Vibrate

I have spoken of energy as another dimension of life. Let's talk some more about this. When You chose to experience being in the physical realm as your *Self*, you were energy. When you were born, and even at the fusion point of the *Mind*, *Body*, and *Self*, as was mentioned before, the *Mind* was already resonating with images, experiences, and vibrations it was organized around from the past. The *Self* is only vibrating in the unfolding of the journey and the impact that You came to make with your life.

For example, the journey You chose is already occurring when you are in the womb. When you are born, you have a *Body*, and the *Mind* is now organizing itself for life. You need to use the *Mind* to learn to live—to discover and be taught how to be and function in the physical paradigm of the world. This energy is what is resonating loudest.

When you awaken to the awareness that you are your *Self* and you have a *Mind*, you shift the frequency in which you resonate and vibrate to now include and activate a new truth—that what is resonating from your *Self* is also real. This "knowing" develops the muscle to bring forth the awareness, that your *Self* is what chose to live and experience the journey that is possible in the physical realm. In this shift in energy—and in how you vibrate and resonate—there are things that occur and arise as a natural flow from your *Self*. Similarly, when you are vibrating and resonating from the *Mind*, there are things that occur and arise that are a natural flow from the patterns and "karmic energies" of the *Mind*.

The bringing forth of your *Self* as who you are can only occur through a choice you make—a conscious choice to know that you have a *Mind*, but it is not who you are. In this you are choosing a new paradigm and a new context, allowing this energy and vibration to activate a new frequency that allows results that cannot occur in the current paradigm. In the energy of the current paradigm, you are a victim of what is occurring in life, because you are dependent on your *Mind*, which has your survival as its dominant energy.

In the energy of *Self*, you are bringing your highest *Self* to life, and there is nothing that is not available to you from your *Self*, for what you are here for is to bring your true and highest, divine nature to the experience of life. Shaping a life that is aligned with the honor of *Self* as a vibration brings forth a oneness with all of life. This is a new paradigm for the planet.

## The Energy and Design of *Self*

Our *Self* is real. It exists as an eternal vibrational essence. The energy of *Self* is designed to always have our Actions come from our divine nature. We each embody a dimension of our *Self* called our *Spirit*. Your *Self* is your *Spirit*. Its design is to ensure you always have a pathway, in any situation, that is an expression of your highest truth. *Self* is about being true to who you are—it is an energy of honor, the honoring of *You* and others.

Imagine that you are nothing but love and oneness, that you embody, in your true nature, the goodness of all things. Your *Self* feels and responds to all energy that is about unconditional love. *Self* is an energy that, when activated, brings out the frequency that aligns your life with your true purpose. Each time you Connect and Act from your *Self* in each moment of "now," you are fulfilling on your *Self's* journey and purpose here this lifetime. The journey of your *Self* is to activate and Act from your *Self* in each moment of "now."

This requires a shift in awareness and living from a new truth that you are not your *Mind* or *Body*—your *Self* is what is real. The experience of the physical dimension creates an illusion that you are your *Mind* and your *Body*. This illusion is designed to allow for the current paradigm to be what you Trust and Act from. Moving from living from the current paradigm that you are your *Mind* requires a shift in awareness of accepting that you are not your *Mind* or your *Body*. This energy requires transcending the *Mind's* paradigm. This shift in awareness is profound and only possible when you choose to release the *Mind* as your truth and to claim your *Self* as who you are. This is a personal and individual choice. No one can make this shift for you.

### A Tool to Begin This Shift in Awareness

- Close your eyes and take a deep breath, relax, and let go of the thoughts coming from the *Mind*.

- Begin to presence your *Self* as Energy; feel it as a vibration.

- Begin at the top of your head and allow the energy and vibration of your *Self* to flow through your *Body* to the bottom of your feet.

- Imagine and presence yourself as an eternal energy that has chosen a physical form.

- Allow this energy to become more and more real.

- Presence the energy as a vibration that encompasses your *Body* until the *Body* is no longer there—just this vibration.

- Imagine yourself as a field of energy, a field of light.

- Be there with You as just energy.

- Hold this as a "knowing" of what is real as You.

(To hear an mp3 audio of this exercise, go to www. indiratoday.com/Books/newparadigm1.)

Once you begin to Connect to your *Self*, you will be pulled into an energy of bringing your *Self* to life around you as your Actions come from *Self*. This will provide a remarkably different experience in how you see yourself, others, and life itself.

The contextual shift in living from this new truth that who you are is not your *Mind* or *Body*, but your *Self*, will create a new paradigm of immense joy and "inner knowing" in your life.

## Embracing Your *Self* as the Journey That Life Is Designed Around

Your *Self* is the engine that drives you to your best life. It is the blueprint for your greatest experience in your physical form. Knowing that your *Self* is a new paradigm allows you to have a unique relationship to what you will Connect, Listen, Trust, and Act from, and this relationship becomes what you honor. When you embrace your *Self* as the journey that life is designed around, each situation becomes a moment to "seek into" what there is to know from your *Self* about what is occurring. You begin to empower your *Self* as a new paradigm.

Imagine that you have a *Self* that is here for a miraculous journey, but this miraculous journey is totally different from what it looks like to have a miraculous journey from the perspective of the *Mind*. The *Mind* and the *Self* are organized around two totally different outcomes and intentions. One is all about what is physical, and this is the *Mind's* view. The *Self's* energy is about having you experience your connectedness to all, to experience innate love, and to honor all of life.

This is where you begin to differentiate knowing your *Self* as You as opposed to your *Mind* as You. When you embrace your *Self* as the journey that your life is designed around, everything in your life shifts its context. Everything is now shaped by the unfolding of the journey of your *Self*.

You begin to see all of what is happening in your journey from the perspective of what has caused this to be part of your journey. When you Connect to your *Self*, you are able to live life from what there is to know from your *Self* about what is unfolding. Without activating this from your *Self*, you will only get what is available from your *Mind*. Part of Connecting to your *Self* to unfold your true journey is transcending the energy of the *Mind*, so it can be a tool used by your *Self* to fulfill the journey, without being the dominant energy that runs your life. It is only through Connecting to your *Self* that you release the *Mind* to continue to Listen, Trust, and Act from your *Self*—knowing that it is through your *Self* that your life will unquestionably be aligned with walking and unfolding your purpose in this lifetime.

Making this choice and empowering this choice is a state change in your relationship to You, life, and the journey. Only you can choose this. Only you can claim this new paradigm. Only you can know this is what you are choosing—for nothing in the current paradigm will call forth such a shift in awareness.

### Karen, Business Consultant

In May of 2005 I was diagnosed with a tumor on my spine and told I had to go in for back surgery. And at the time I was just starting to learn to Connect, and I wasn't very conscious of the *Mind*. I had had a pain in my back for about two years and asked the doctors to look into it. They did all the normal x-rays and then treated me for a bunch of funny things like acid reflux, pneumonia, cracked ribs—real strange things. They didn't find anything. Finally they did an MRI, and we discovered the tumor on my spinal cord and that was a total shock to me. I don't know what I expected, but I certainly didn't expect that. They wanted to operate within four or five days of finding that, but I said no, I wanted a second opinion, because I just couldn't believe that I would have a tumor. I went to another doctor for it, a surgeon. I met with this surgeon, and I took all my x-rays and MRIs to him and he told me that it was a tumor, and that he would be able to operate on it. So I set the surgery up with him. After he did the surgery, he told me that it was much more difficult than he thought it was going to be and the tumor was much bigger than what he saw on the x-ray. The reality was that if he hadn't operated on it, in about thirty days I would have been paralyzed by it. He felt I was very lucky because typically these types of tumors are

*(continued)*

silent tumors and don't normally have any pain or warning or anything associated with them. He said, "Typically I don't see patients with this type of tumor until they are in a wheelchair." I said, "But what about the pain in my back?" He said it was totally unrelated to the tumor. It was just muscular pain. It was due to my posture and how I was holding myself. After all of the surgery and the recovery, I still had the pain. It took me eighteen months to fully recover from the surgery. Interestingly enough, I had started to work on Connecting with Indira about five months before that, and she told me right away that one of the first things I was going to end up working on was my health and well-being, and that was what there was to take care of. And this was before I found out about the tumor and everything.

I actually ended up getting several surgeries—three surgeries in four months. So my true recovery didn't really start until December. And by that time I felt down and out; prior to the third surgery, I couldn't even walk. My leg had gone completely spastic, so I was in a wheelchair, and I was facing being in a wheelchair for the rest of my life. There was just no place in my *Mind* that I could go to handle this, so I went to Connecting to my *Self* instead. I started to Connect a lot, and I kept getting this statement from my *Self*, "You're going to be alright, you're going to be alright." From my *Mind*, I had a hard time Trusting that. But that just kept coming through, "You're going to be alright." I really was up against feeling like there was nowhere to go except Connecting to my *Self*. Indira had Connected as well and sent me a message that said that I could Trust my *Self* and I could Trust what I was getting, and that I was here to walk that journey. I read that message over and over again. I was on a lot of medication, lying flat on my back, and I was scared out of my mind. There was a lot going wrong physi-cally for me, I had spinal fluid leakage, and I had a scar-tissue block down my spine and was in a lot of pain. Through all of that, I just kept reading that message and Trusting it. It was very difficult. My *Mind* was going crazy, but I think, like so many people when they are in crisis, I had nowhere to go but to *Spirit*. All along I just kept Trusting what I was getting. I kept Connecting and getting Actions to take. So the first Action I got to take was to walk, just walk on the treadmill to build up the strength in my back. And that was so hard, and I didn't want to do it because it was so painful. Especially the first five minutes was really painful, but when I got off the treadmill, I felt so much better. So I knew my *Self* was right, and now I Trust what I get when I Connect. The experience of hearing my *Self* gets more and more pronounced the more I do it. I can now recognize what my *Self* sounds like and differentiate it from my *Mind*. There's a lot of peace around it, and there's a "knowing" that it will all turn out. Whatever it is, it will all turn out. There's nothing that I *have* to do, but there's everything that I *can* do. It leaves me very energized. There's an urgency to be in life and to have every experience I can have. That's how it's altered my life, and that's huge.

## How Living from Your *Self* Reshapes Who You Are and Why You Are Here

Having your Actions come from your *Self* is a journey of Trusting your *Self* as who you are and knowing that the choice to be here is for a specific intention. Choosing to live from your *Self* is a choice to honor that You are here for a specific journey—the one that is from your *Self*.

It is presencing a new paradigm that even while you are embracing a physical existence, the real reason you exist is to Connect, Listen, Trust, and Act on what is being communicated from your *Self* as your true reality.

When you step into that, you become the source of all that you need to know in any situation. You become the manifestation of what You came to impart and contribute to the world by having the gift to be in a physical form. This contribution is not from the view of the current paradigm, it is from the view of what there is in the next moment that honors your *Self* and another person's *Self*.

When people Connect to their higher *Self* and live from this new paradigm, we will begin to reshape what the world is about and how we can be with each other, where life itself is now an expression of our *Self*. Situations become a moment to choose compassion, love, forgiveness, and oneness, as the driver of our lives. Where we work, what we do, how we live will become the secondary dimension of our lives. What occurs is that those things that we need to be comfortable and enjoy life naturally unfold in our lives. When we Connect, Listen, Trust, and Act from our *Self*, all of what we need to exist in the physical realm becomes a *part* of the journey—not *the* journey—which is how it appears to be from the current paradigm.

There is a shift in how things around you occur. You see them through the lens of your *Self* first. You experience life in the duality of the energy of the *Mind* and of the *Self*. You embrace and begin to Trust, your intuitive nature as a guide that is there to ensure you live from a "knowing" that all is well, all is as it should be, as a new context for life. You become a human being who is emulating divine presence and whose life is an expression of what brings a higher vibration and frequency to the planet.

Your Trust becomes more natural and effortless. Your Trust of the journey becomes the Connection, as you release fear, concern, worry, and the *Mind's* drive to use up your time in the illusion that there is someplace to get to.

You will begin to exude an energy of strength in your truth and in knowing that you are on an eternal journey. You will relate to the people around you from the "set-up" you have to be with them this lifetime. You have your job be where you are in the "now" as you honor what is there from your *Self* in the face of any and all circumstances.

The quality of life is altered. While you are in the physical realm, you are not of the physical realm; you are existing in a new vibration of being a spiritual being on a spiritual journey.

## Redefining Your Relationship to Your *Self* as Who You Are

Choosing to know who you are as your *Self* is a decision to claim your *Self* as your reality, distinct from your *Mind*. The redefining of your *Self* as who you are is a new pathway to a new paradigm for life to exist in.

When life exists inside of this redefinition of who you are, you have activated the vibration of your highest divine nature as You. What you do in each moment becomes a powerful access point to a new you—a You that you know you came here to manifest.

When your Actions in life are aligned with the journey of your *Self*, you begin to experience a natural flow in life. You tend to engage in what there is to do in the physical world, not from a need to survive, but from an honoring of what is needed in life to fulfill your true *Self*. You become aligned in an energy, a vibration, a frequency that allows you to have things, events, situations, and circumstances arise to support that journey. Each day is a new moment from which to choose your *Self* as real. This choice is the gift of life. This choice redefines what life is designed for as you begin to live your life from the eternal nature of the journey. This shifts what impels you to make the choices you do; the force comes not from the *Mind's* dynamics, but from a Trusting of your *Self*. As such, you transcend the energy of getting to a destination and start to embody the duality of *Self* and *Mind*, knowing that the *Mind* is an access to your journey, but it is not the journey itself.

In this new paradigm shift, life slows down. There is no need to get somewhere, to accomplish something. All that there is to focus on is to Connect, Listen, Trust, and Act from your *Self*. When you do this, you become organized around that as your reality—for it is in these four steps that You arise, claim your *Self*, and bring forth who there is to be, as a human being.

### The Patterns of Your *Self*: Your *Self* as an Eternal Energy

You are an eternal energy called *Self*. You vibrate and resonate with the "knowing" of your True and Highest *Self*, an energy of universal consciousness that is powerful and real. The eternal nature of your *Self* allows you to activate dimensions within you that transcend the current paradigm. Your experiences in your eternal journey vibrate and resonate in your DNA for who you really are—an eternal energy.

As energy, you have dimensions of yourself that resonate and vibrate, evoking truths from your true *Self*. The eternal nature of your *Self* allows you to always have within you, as energy, an "inner knowing" that will guide your experience to its fullest self-expression.

Knowing that you are energy—you are eternal and you vibrate with the "knowing" of your highest *Self*— allows you to know that within you is everything you need to Act in any and all situations. This "knowing" is the eternal energy called your *Self*.

## Recognizing Your *Self* as a Vibration— How to Activate This Journey

You activate the journey of your *Self* by recognizing that you *have* a *Self*. It is real. It is eternal. It is who you are.

By choosing to know that your *Self* is as real, as strong, and as powerful a source for your life as your *Mind*, you bring into existence an "inner knowing" that shifts you from the current paradigm into the new paradigm.

When you activate a new truth that the energy of your *Self* is who you are, you are shifting from one paradigm to another. You are choosing to have your *Self* be the dominant vibration you are willing to Trust as You.

Your *Self* is always vibrating at a frequency that evokes your highest truth. Therefore, anytime you Connect, Listen, Trust, and Act from your *Self*, your Actions will always unfold your life in alignment with your best life. What you will confront is the *Mind's* drive to keep you in the logic and fear the *Mind* presences to keep you acting from the *Mind*. But from your *Self*, it is the Trusting of what you get to Act on that becomes the catalyst for your best life.

This journey requires a Trust in knowing that you have a *Self* that is real, tangible, and what chose to be in your physical form. It also activates the "inner knowing" that the *Mind* is here to be a tool for the journey of your *Self*.

As you Trust and Act from your *Self*, you will confront and release the *Mind*, creating a duality of *Mind* and *Self* as a new paradigm.

Developing this relationship with your *Self* will allow you to live in the "knowing" that your journey as a human being is to experience your best life. It is not elusive. It is not unattainable. Rather, it is resonating in each moment as you switch from your *Mind's* energy as who you are to your *Self's* energy as who you are.

## Your *Self* as a "Radio Station" That Is Always On, Communicating Your Highest Intentions

Your *Self* is always vibrating in the "knowing" of all that is and all that exists energetically. Much like you experience when tuning into a radio station, this *Self* "radio station" is always on, communicating what there is for you to know at any moment of "now" about all that is occurring and unfolding so that your Actions can come from what is being evoked. Because it is always transmitting, you can choose to Connect and Listen to your *Self* at any time.

It is in this "knowing" that all exists—all that is eternal in nature and of energy—that you find a paradigm shift for why you are here. You don't have to figure it out from your *Mind*. You can simply Connect to the "radio station" of *Self* and Listen for what is there for you to know about what is occurring now in your journey. This is where you will bring forth the life *You* came here to experience. This duality allows for having your *Self* be as great as what your *Mind* is creating as its paradigm.

## Life in the New Paradigm: Organized around Your *Self*'s Intentions, What Is Being Evoked from *Self* Is Real

Living in a new paradigm means living from your *Self* and Connecting to your *Self* for all you need to know in life. Life in the new paradigm is a life where what you get from your *Self* is what you Trust and Act on. These Actions are not at all in sync with what your *Mind* will be driven to act on. The Actions you get to take from your *Self* will be about what works for everyone and for the honor of your highest *Self* and each other's highest *Self*. It is a very different paradigm—one where it will be impossible to dishonor another person, to operate from a place of separation, and instead will be naturally living from new truths that redefine why you are here.

Yes, you will need to make money and survive, but this energy will be secondary to honoring the journey of your *Self*'s intentions—what your *Self* is here to experience, unfold, and fulfill. You will find new ways to handle situations. For example, when you are angry, you will find that *Self* gives you ways to operate that will honor your *Self* while at the same time honoring the highest *Self* in the person you are angry with. This gives you the opportunity to experience win-win situations with all of the relationships in your life. You will discover other pathways to what's important. Your *Self* knows what this journey is really about. Your *Self*'s energy and vibration will be what arises in the experience of your life.

This is clearly a new paradigm. As you go to Connect to your *Self* for what there is to know and Act on in any and all situations, you begin to activate an energy that aligns you with your purpose and journey. This, as energy, shifts the energy around you to one of honoring life. In the honoring of all life—your *Self* and the *Self* of each other—the Actions you take only forward the new paradigm.

This new paradigm will unfold a world, and how we see each other shifts from one of acting from what is real to the *Mind*—which is a vibration of separation and fear—to Trusting and Acting on what is real from our *Self*—which is a vibration of oneness and connectedness.

You will find yourself in two distinct realms—one driven by the *Mind* and one driven by your *Self*. You will experience a distinct life in which there is a natural and effortless unfolding to what you are guided to do and be. This is the journey of your *Self*.

Within this new energy of your *Self* you begin to experience life differently. You begin to transcend fear of what is occurring around you, of life itself, of never making it, of never having enough time, money, possessions, love, or control. You can get beyond whatever the *Mind* has decided it is time to fear. It is that simple.

You will be within the energy of a collective consciousness, the universal "knowing" of your oneness as your truth, called your *Self*. You will know that by simply perceiving your *Self* as who you are you have opened a pathway to a different life. You have altered the paradigm from which you exist as your *Mind* to trusting life. You bring to life your true *Self*. You bring to life the experience of honor in any and all situations. You become the catalyst you came here to be and experience.

## Donna, President and Director of a
## Video Production Company

A beloved great-aunt of mine had just died at the age of 102. For many years she and her sister (who had died two years before also at 102) had been telling me how much money I was going to get in the trust when they died and what they wanted me to use that money for, which was to buy a house. My father was the executor of the trust, and when he picked my brother and me up at the airport to attend the funeral, he started to talk about the trust and how much he thought we were going to be getting. It was less than what the aunts had been telling us, and my brother and I were upset about this but didn't know how to deal with it. My brother mentioned it briefly in the car, and my father told him he didn't know the exact amounts yet so not to worry about it. But when we were alone, my brother and I discussed how upset we were about the whole thing. We were afraid to just ask to see the paperwork, because we thought it would seem like we didn't trust my father. My family history on my father's side includes a lot of people not speaking to each other for years out of anger, and we really didn't want this to happen over our aunt's trust. But this left us not knowing what to do. My *Mind* was very loud about it. It kept saying loudly that this was going to be a mess, that to accept the money as it was without questioning it would mean resenting the situation forever after. But my *Mind* was also just as loud about the fact that it thought if I questioned my father about it, he would think I didn't trust him or something and he would get angry and never speak to me again. It was very sure about both things, which

*(continued)*

painted me into a corner and paralyzed my actions. I started Connecting to my *Self*, but my *Mind* was very loud and for several weeks all I could do was work at quieting my *Mind*, which was more like being really aware of the *Mind's* control in this situation. It was loud, strong, and powerful in stating that I was being "screwed" and I would lose my father. A solution popped up from my *Mind* and it said if I could just get a copy of the will by finding out the name of the lawyer, then I could discover what it said without my father knowing, and then I would know what I needed to know and he wouldn't get mad. But I had a nagging feeling that this was a *Mind*-generated solution. It felt sneaky and wrong, so instead I just kept Connecting every morning when I got up and every night before going to bed. I was in turmoil. Finally I got a clear message from *Self* that said, "You don't really know what the trust says or what your father is doing in executing it. Let it go, wait and see what happens. Trust that all will be well." So I did. I kept Connecting every morning and every night about it. Then I would go about my day. I tried not to think about it. From my *Mind* it still felt like a dire situation. Families get torn apart over wills on a daily basis, and I didn't want that to happen. This went on for two months, and I went through a lot of pain during that time. I bounced back and forth between being angry at feeling this way and being terrified that I was going to lose my father or my brother over the situation. Finally, right before Christmas I saw my father, and he gave me an inheritance check. It was more than he had said at the airport, but less than my aunts had told me it would be. I didn't say anything, as I still didn't know what to do or say about it; after all, it was still a generous amount of money. I said nothing, but I knew my father knew I wasn't quite happy about it. Luckily he didn't question me then. When he gave my brother his check a week later, my brother did question him about it and asked to see the trust and talk to the lawyer. He did a great job of saying all the right things, and my father didn't get angry at all and patiently explained everything to him. A few weeks later when we were together for my father's birthday, he asked me if I had any questions about the inheritance because he said he could tell from my face when he gave me the check that I wasn't happy about it. I told him my brother had told me most of it and he repeated to me what he had told my brother. To my surprise, I found out what really happened that had the amount be different than what I was told. Despite that the aunts had been telling me and my brother specific monetary figures and stock certificates we would get, the fact was that they had had to set up the trust in percentages instead of specific money figures. In any case, it was clear that he had followed the trust's guidelines to a fault and the money we had gotten was exactly what it was supposed to be, but he still offered to show me the trust and give me the lawyer's contact information, without my asking for it. I was so glad in that moment that I had trusted what I had gotten from Connecting to my *Self*, because all really was as it was supposed to be.

## How Your Life Will Shift When Living from Your *Self* as You

The experience of your life when lived from your *Self* is a new view of what we are all doing here. You will begin to view life, each moment and all situations, through the lens of what there is to know about this from your *Self*. You will know that no matter what is occurring, it is powerfully connected to why you chose to have that experience. Each experience is yours to have in transcending the *Mind* to truly Connect, Listen, Trust, and Act from your *Self*.

You will be within the journey, free to let go of everything the *Mind* has determined is real, because that is how it exists in the current paradigm. You will make bold changes. You will experience being fearless. You will know yourself as a part of the whole, and you will let go of everything the *Mind* has determined is real.

You will quickly and effortlessly move through the *Mind's* drive to continue keeping you separate, distant, removed, judgmental, fearful, and dishonoring to finding yourself honoring, loving, forgiving, being compassionate, and having your Actions create a oneness with the people in your life.

## The Impact on Humanity When We Live from the New Paradigm—Our *Self* Is Who We Are

We will reshape what it means to be a human being to include that we are a spiritual being on a spiritual journey. This shift will bring us to new thoughts about what is important. We will find ourselves within the vibration of love, forgiveness, fairness, and all those qualities that call forth who we truly are—honoring and loving to ourselves and each other. We will reveal a new paradigm. We will reshape how we confront conflicts. We will have a new awareness of how our speaking leaves others. The system in which life is organized from the current paradigm will no longer be how we see and live life. How we see each other's differences will shift as we bring forth from within our *Self* a new experience of how life can be lived.

The pathway to living this new paradigm is to Connect, Listen, Trust, and Act from your *Self*. As I have mentioned, when you Connect, Listen, Trust, and Act from your *Self*, you bring yourself into the vibration, frequency, and resonance of your highest *Self*. This is the *Self* that is here for who you truly are and what your journey is designed around during this period of being in a physical form.

In the four steps of Connecting, Listening, Trusting, and Acting, you switch the track your life is on, from one of being driven by your *Mind* to one of being your *Self*. As you experience this shift in the two dimensions of your being human, you bring yourself into the truth of who you really are—a spiritual being on a spiritual journey. You create a new paradigm where life is the gift for being on your eternal journey of knowing your *Self*.

As energy you exist in a vibrational force of resonance, evoking the truth of your divine *Self*. In a *Body* and having a *Mind*, you get to experience your *Self*. The journey of life is to experience this *Self* in your relationships with others, your family members, your life partner. It is also the experience of the diversity of what you look like on the outside, in the *Body* you came into, with each of us being different colors, different sizes, with different ways of being and living. When you shift from the paradigm of the *Mind* to the paradigm of Listening to *Self*, you recognize that this is simply the cover you wear. We are all on an eternal journey. We are all one day leaving our physical form and the physical plane. This energy as a truth vibrates from your *Self*, it shapes the energy from which you get to have your Actions come from when you Connect, Listen, Trust, and Act from your *Self*.

You shape the journey of life from your innate magnificence. In each moment of "now" you have a choice of where your Actions will come from. You become someone living from your *Self* naturally, and the *Mind's* need to pull you into situations to "feel" Connected to your *Self* is no longer required. You will find yourself seeking to be Connected to your *Self* as the pathway to your best life, knowing that your *Self* is the source of your best life in any situation. The practice of Connecting, Listening, Trusting, and Acting from your *Self* as a way of life becomes the journey you will tend to and honor.

## ~ 4 ~

# Connect: Accessing the Communication from *Self*

Connecting is the first step in bringing forth a shift into the new paradigm of living from your *Self*. In this new paradigm, your *Self* becomes the "radio station" that you are tuned into to guide your actions in life. Connecting is the step of unplugging the *Mind's* energy to activate the energy of your *Self*. When you begin to Connect, you align how you vibrate and resonate with that of your *Self*—the source of all "knowing." This shift allows the realm of energy to become real in your human experience. You become aligned with the vibrational force that holds the earth and the planets and all that exists as energy in the universe. You begin to resonate and vibrate as you really are—an eternal energetic force of higher consciousness. To Connect is to activate this frequency, this energy, as real and available to you.

There is no new paradigm without Connecting. You are, by your human nature, connected to your *Mind* as who you are. Your *Mind* controls your experience and your actions in the physical world. How you act and why you make the choices you do in any situation are given by the *Mind's* view of life around you. In some cultures some actions are considered normal, whereas in other cultures those same actions are bizarre. The *Mind* shapes how you should think and feel about what is happening.

When you Connect to your *Self* for the answers that are unique to you, through the question—"What is there for me to know?"—you are surrendering to a new truth that you are not your *Mind*. The act of Connecting is the core to living a new paradigm, given that Connecting is the release of the *Mind* as the gatekeeper to your reality. The moment you take the step to Connect you have altered your reality. You are claiming your *Self* as the source of your journey. Connecting is the step that puts you within the new paradigm.

### Activating the Duality—The Reason to Connect

Connecting activates the duality of the *Mind* and the *Self*. You exist in a duality given both your *Mind* and your *Self* are always a part of how you experience your life. You activate this duality when you Connect, for with this act you are presencing your *Self* as a dimension of you that is real. The duality of *Mind* and *Self* as a way of life becomes possible when you are living from the new paradigm of energy.

The *Mind* will always be active and always a driver of life. It is designed to ensure your survival and to keep you powerfully connected to the physical world. Knowing that there will always be the journey of the *Mind* allows you to also hold that there is a journey of your *Self*, that is separate and distinct from the *Mind*. This is the duality—to have both as an awareness and to choose to bring forth your *Self* in all situations. You do this knowing that it is from your *Self* that you honor yourself and the *Self* of another, as the gift you are here to experience.

It is through Connecting that you bring forth a new awareness of your *Self* as separate from your *Mind*. Not as a concept, but as a new paradigm called energy—the energy of your *Self*. This new paradigm presences a new experience of what life is about and why you are here.

In the current paradigm we fit into what is in the world. From the *Mind*, we look outside ourselves for the answers to belong and fit in. Unaware of the realm of energy as a dimension of us that impacts how we live, we find ourselves disconnected from our *Self* as the *Mind* continues to create our life. In this disconnect many people find themselves searching elusively for the experience of their *Self*, for their energy is now vibrating in alignment with wanting to experience who they really are. However, the current paradigm is not designed to access our *Self*.

Connecting is the pathway to shift away from the *Mind* as your reality. When you Connect to your *Self* and ask, "What is there for me to know about (any situation)?" you are saying that what is occurring from your *Mind* is *not* your reality. You are saying that your journey is to Listen for what is being communicated from your *Self* and to honor that as real. You are saying that you know you are an eternal energy of divine consciousness and that whatever is occurring is the journey you came to walk and transcend, i.e., the *Mind's* views and truth about what is happening. Connecting has your actions come from your *Self* not from what the world has determined is the action to take in that situation. Perhaps most important, through Connecting you alter your vibration and resonance to align with the Universal "knowing" and your *Self's* journey in this lifetime. This journey shapes what is important and necessary in the experience of your life. You will not be driven by the *Mind* to do things to fit in, to make it, and to belong. You will be at home in the energy of your *Self*. This is the power of Connecting!

## Developing Your Power to Connect

To Connect you are making a conscious choice to stop life and align with your *Self* now. In a similar way to meditation, you are quieting your *Mind*. But Connecting takes it a step further in that once your *Mind* is quiet, you will not simply sit in that silence. Instead you will activate communication with your eternal *Self* for the answers that are unique to you. This is simply different than when you are living from the answers you get from your *Mind*. This is a new practice to take on to live your life in the new paradigm. It is a practice that then becomes a way of life. Much like a baby learning to walk, it takes practicing Connecting often and frequently in your day-to-day life.

In the beginning it may be that you are setting aside time to Connect on a weekly or biweekly basis. But as you develop your access to your *Self* through Connecting often, it will become as natural as breathing. You will find that the channel of your *Self* is a tone and vibration and resonance that you easily and naturally recognize as your *Self*—distinct from your *Mind*.

The practice of Connecting trains you to Listen for the difference between the energy of your *Mind* and the energy of your *Self*. When you begin to know this as a difference in energy and vibration, you will be able to know when your *Mind* is presencing something distinct from what your *Self* presences. Your *Self* is always in communication with you about what there is to know in any situation: now you can Listen for what that is and Act on it.

## Unplugging the *Mind*

The practice of Connecting is the practice of unplugging the *Mind*. As energy, our *Mind* is plugged into every dimension of our actions in the physical world. Through our five senses we are always powerfully related to the sounds, sights, touch, and taste of life—it keeps us ON all the time as human beings. Our innate need to belong, to live with all of what we need to do in our daily lives to survive, becomes the platform from which the *Mind* is at work. It never stops, and now with the new technologies we have, such as cell phones with Internet access, we are using the *Mind* even more to not only function in the physical world but also in the technological world. All our social media sites and ways of communicating and the global shift in having everything available to us at our fingertips are revolutionizing the power and control of the *Mind*. We have more of our *Mind* determining more of our daily life. One of the general complaints these days is that people say they cannot focus or relax because their *Mind* is always racing and it is always engaged with the constant flow of information that is being taken in through all the technologies at hand. Most people cannot even check the time on their cell phones without becoming totally engaged with their email, text messages, news feeds, and more. And all of this keeps the *Mind* churning and churning, never allowing us to relax or turn it all off, even for a moment. This way of living is dredging up new issues we find ourselves dealing with, such as not being able to sleep, becoming addicted as a way to check out, etc.

The *Mind's* relationship to reality has shifted dramatically in the past decade. What is real through these new technological venues, which allow us to see video and pictures, as well as text and graphics, and which "feed" us all of it automatically, is seen by the *Mind* as truths. For example, the *Mind* creates that reading a profile and seeing a picture or video of someone on a website is as real as having them in front of us—our emotions are evoked as naturally as if we had seen them physically. So then, how can you know if someone is conning you over that website or if they are even the person they say they are? It is very difficult due to the fact that the *Mind* is shaping what is occurring as real because that is the way the *Mind* processes situations——through our five physical senses.

But, what if you had a sixth sense? People often talk about the sixth sense, your intuition, but few people feel like they can access that sixth sense when they need it, and as such we usually feel as though it is just luck that that "gut feeling" stopped us from doing something foolish, or nudged us to take the right action at the right time. This sixth sense, or your intuitive moment, is actually the energy of your *Self*. We have all heard it at one time or another, but few people have learned how to harness its power and live life from it. Connecting allows you to use your *Self* as a radar for what is real: It comes to the situation from a different vibration and therefore tunes you into a part of you that is on the track for your true and highest *Self*. In this vibration you will activate the "intuitive You" such that all of what the *Mind* is attempting to unfold will shift to what your *Self* is here to unfold. In this journey communicating with a con artist cannot exist, because the energy of the situation and the energy of your *Self* will simply not have the exchange happen.

Through Connecting you begin to have a new awareness of who you truly are. As you begin to Listen, Trust, and Act from Connecting to your *Self*, your actions are now very different from what the *Mind* has your actions be about. You will naturally find yourself taking actions that bring an honoring to life around you. You begin to know yourself differently. The *Self* is a "knowing" that resonates within you cellularly, and this will begin to be expressed outside of you in the world around you. No longer is the *Mind* the only thing determining your actions and your experience of life.

This awareness will have you release old energies that span lifetimes. You will begin to Trust in the innate intuitive *Self* that guides you to Act in ways that are many times opposed to what the *Mind's* energy is designed around. You will experience being able to release control and release the innate need to protect yourself from situations that from the *Mind* you think may hurt you or have you experience not being honored. In other words you will be seeing everything through your journey and the "set-up" you have designed, and you will start to transcend your *Mind's* views and truths.

All of life is brought forth no matter your age, your background, your socioeconomic status when you are operating from a foundation of your *Self*. You move through the *Mind's* relationship to who you are in the physical world. How you see people of all stages of life and all ages and all races/colors and all backgrounds becomes not a function of what your *Mind* sees and knows but rather what your highest *Self* is here to presence and make real.

It is in this new paradigm you experience being whole, rather than struggling with the *Mind's* energy of always having to fix yourself in some way in order to survive. It is truly a new paradigm in the "knowing" of who you are. It dissipates the experience of being separate and alone to be replaced by the divine nature of your *Self* as the paradigm you live from.

## Linda, Sales Representative

Here's how I know when I'm in the *Mind's* energy: it says "I want, I need, I have to have." Those are the things that pop up, and they are the *Mind* telling me that I should do this or I shouldn't do that, and it sounds distinctly different from anything the *Self* tells me. When my *Mind* has kicked in about something that has upset me, first I have to realize that it's happened, and for me it usually means that I feel diminished in some way, or threatened, and I feel like I have to defend myself. Somebody has said something or done something that makes my *Mind* react in a certain way where it wants to win, it wants to feel better, so a lot of times the way to feel better is to put that other person down or somehow making them wrong so that I can be right and maintain this identity of the *Mind*. And that's a tough thing to disengage from because of the years of conditioning and routine of reacting that way, but as soon as I feel that I *have* to fight back, I know I'm in my *Mind's* energy. So for example with my husband, when he does something that pushes my buttons, immediately I feel like I should push back, but now I can step back and I can let go of so much more of the right and wrong, which is so subjective, and really Listen to my *Self* with regard to detaching from whatever it was we were arguing about. I can look at it as, "Is it really worth it getting into this whole pattern of fight and you know that whole cycle of whatever the *Mind* puts me through that I try to win?" And it's often something that doesn't even really matter in the end. So the feeling of diminishment, that feeling in the beginning of "Okay, if I don't fight, and I don't stand up for what I want, I'm losing," turns into an expansion instead. But I have to feel that *Mind* energy first—I can't just push it away, I have to just allow it to be there—and then my *Self* allows it to be in this kind of container of spaciousness, the space that's beyond the *Mind*. That space of *Self* usually says, "Do you want to be right, or do you want to not have a fight right now? Do you want to change the energy into something that's negative, or do you want to let this go and see what happens?" And when I let it go, all of a sudden it does change the energy, and my husband feels it too because I'm not fighting back, I'm not pushing his buttons. While he doesn't even know this is all happening, something shifts as my energy shifts from my *Mind* to my *Self*, even though he does not Connect. But that doesn't matter because the energy still permeates through his *Mind*, and he is able then to have his energy match mine, and we drop it. It's pointless. But it all comes from the energy of it. I'm releasing the *Mind's* energy in the moment, and it changes the energy between us.

## Living in the Now

When your life is lived from the energy of your *Self*, the frequency in which you vibrate and resonate emits a vibration that disconnects anything that is not aligned with the energy of your True and Highest *Self*. Your energetic force aligns your life with what there is to know, at any moment, to live in the honoring of all life. This is the "radio station" that is always on, resonating and vibrating in the frequency of your true and highest *Self*.

When you are tuned into the "radio station" of your *Self*, you are not living in the fear of what could happen or what might happen: you are in the energy of your eternal journey, and this is what disengages the *Mind* as your paradigm. The *Mind's* energy is always about surviving in this lifetime, but the *Self* is always in the awareness that you are eternal and that your journey is also eternal. It resonates in a vibration of "all is well, all is as it should be." As such, your journey of your *Self* exists in the "now," or said another way, in the present moment. In the energy of your *Self* there is no past or future. Each moment is a new moment to activate your *Self* for what your experience in life in that moment is designed to presence to bring forth as your journey. This is the energy you are activating when you choose to Connect to the "radio station" vibrating as your *Self*.

When you are tuned into your *Self*, you are always in the "now," in the "knowing" that being in your *Body*, and living life from your *Mind*, is not what being here is about. In this new vibration, you have access to Connecting to your *Self* for what there is to know about your journey in *any* moment. Living in the "now" is not the design of the *Mind*. It only exists in the energy of your *Self*. In a "now" you have direct access to energy as real. In a "now" you live in the totality of all that exists eternally. This allows for a level of calmness and peace few people ever experience.

Connecting is putting yourself in that paradigm. Having that paradigm available to you allows you to relate to each situation for the unfolding of the life YOU came to experience in this lifetime. In these experiences the choice to Act from your *Self* distinct from your *Mind* allows for the energy of your *Self* to be who you resonate as, and in this resonance you are bringing a higher frequency and vibration to earth. You are the one that shifts the experience of life. You bring an honoring to everything around you.

## Honoring You as Your Highest *Self*

The most powerful act of Connecting is that it is you honoring You. If You are your *Self*—the one that chose a *Mind* and a *Body* to experience itself—then Connecting is simply you honoring You. Imagine you chose to be here to experience the joy of the journey that your *Self* knows it is here for, *but* the moment you are born your life is mostly experienced from your *Mind*. The pull of a human being is to be *Mind*-driven. To claim your journey and your life requires you to have access to your *Self*.

This *is* why your *Self* chose this lifetime—to have an experience of a life, lived from knowing who you truly are, taking actions from this "knowing" of the eternalness of *Self*, vibrating with the truth that we are all connected. There is no other way to know this as an experience. As energy we are in the "knowing" of our *Self*, we are in the "knowing" of this strong and magnificent being. It is only in the honoring of the You that chose this journey that you activate an energy that holds the eternal nature of your journey. In the eternal vibration of your *Self*, you come to know yourself as your *Self*. You become someone that knows that the honoring of YOU is what will have you have your best life. You become someone that becomes organized in the honoring of You as who you are.

We are in an energy where the honoring of our *Self* is what the world is now here to be organized around. Imagine that you chose to have a journey to experience the magnificence of your *Self*, and then you spend your whole life honoring your *Mind*. This misalignment has become more pronounced with the evolution of technological media and as we move into a new era when our interconnectedness is critical to our survival as a planet. For the past three decades humanity has had a shift in energy allowing more access to the energy that vibrates as our *Self*. However, given the current paradigm is *not* designed to honor our *Self* or others, how do we deal with situations and challenges to keep the honoring of each other in place?

It begins with having a relationship to honoring yourself. The *only* way to honor your *Self* is to Connect to your *Self* for what there is to Act on—it is *only* then are you honoring You.

What is being evoked in a Connection? The energy, vibration, and frequency of your *Self*. Connecting is the activation of You as energy. As we discussed in the chapter on conception, You chose to fuse with your *Mind* and your *Body* for this experience. When you Connect, you are shifting from a view that the physical dimension of life is what is real to acknowledging that the realm of energy is what is real. You are beginning to recognize that *everything* is energy.

You are acknowledging that You resonate and vibrate at a frequency that ignites your highest divine nature. This energy is given to us by our breath. As long as this energy is pulsating and vibrating within our cells, we are alive in our *Body*. When this energy is no longer resonating in our *Body*, we are no longer in a physical form, but we still exist and we are real and tangible as energy. You can Connect at any time to the energy of people alive or with those no longer in their *Body*. This is a dimension of the realm of energy.

When you can relate to the dimension of your *Self* as real, you can ignite energy, you can shift energy, you can Connect to the energy for what it is presencing, and you will recognize whether it is aligned with your *Self* or your *Mind*.

It is *all* your choice to live from your *Mind* or your *Self* as what is real. This is the paradigm You chose when You chose to be once again in a *Body*: to know your *Self* as what is real, to bring forth the journey of being a spiritual being on a spiritual journey.

The act of Connecting is you surrendering to this new truth that You are your *Self*. It is acknowledging this truth as your reality. It is acknowledging and shifting energetically how your cells are vibrating. When your cells are vibrating in the "knowing" that resonates in this new truth, you have a whole new access to how you live life. You can transcend the *Mind's* energy on aging, by knowing you have direct access to the energy of your *Body*—its vibration and frequency. This gives you access to healing your *Body* by shifting energy. You bring forth healing, forgiveness, and compassion in the face of the *Mind's* truth about how life is, such that you experience the vastness of your *Self*.

When we all start to relate to everything as energy and that energy can be shifted through this awareness, we become the divine beings we are designed to be while in our physical form. We emulate the divine nature of our true *Self*. We become the *Self* that is yearning to experience itself. We don't live where the *Mind* is playing out a life of reoccurring situations that leave us in an experience of hopelessness or loss of affinity and zest for our best life. Rather than taking our last breath in fear and in the energy of the *Mind's* truth—that our physical paradigm is why we came here—we leave having been in the experience of a life that unfolded from what lived in our Soul.

## An Activation of the *Self* as Real

Connecting is the activation of the *Self* as real. While I have stated this many times, it cannot be said enough, because the *Mind* is simply *not* designed to hold this as a truth. Activation of the *Self* as real is a paradigm shift. It redefines what it means to be a human being. It puts into motion the energy aligned with the statement—You are a spiritual being on a spiritual journey, and it has this energy be what is now resonating as a truth cellularly.

Having your *Self* be what is real shifts your paradigm. Your paradigm will now be aligned with a distinct set of truths about life, what you are here for, and why your being here is Connected to the journey of your *Self*.

This paradigm shift begins to give you access to hearing your *Self* as naturally as you do your *Mind*. This starts shifting the *Mind* into a new role: one of being in service for the journey of your *Self*. This paradigm shift reshapes how you think, what you get organized around in your life, how your relationships occur, what you choose to act on daily in your life, how you see and feel and act on the journey you have while you are in your *Body* this lifetime.

It also reshapes the experience of life from a destination to an eternal journey. How often have you experienced thinking that if you could just get that job, that house, that spouse, then you could be happy in life, only to find out that once you accomplished the goal, you still felt empty inside? If you could just make X amount of money every year, you thought you could finally relax, but then you discover that when you are making that amount, it still doesn't feel like it's enough. If you could just rise to that particular position in your career, everything would be right in the world; only you get there and discover that you still feel unfulfilled, something is still missing. When you Connect to life as an eternal journey, all of what happens is simply unfolding your journey and your impact in the world. There is a state change where life no longer occurs as a destination to get to. Each situation becomes an opportunity to seek into knowing what there is for you to discover, from Self, about what is arising. You are always choosing what is happening as exactly what should happen for it *is* what is occurring "now" in the journey. In this state change there is an experience of peace and ease and a natural "knowing" that "all is well." The anxiety and worry disappear. This "knowing" transcends the physical to embrace a new energy whereby you bring your *Self* to life and shape life from who you *are* distinct from where the *Mind* thinks you should be going or doing.

Activating your *Self* as real allows you to have access to the dimensions of "Universal Energy" where your energy can be a catalyst for shifting your relationships and changing the energy of a situation, simply through altering the vibrational tone and resonance to one that is aligned with your true *Self*.

Activating your *Self* as real shifts the experience of life from fear, concern, worry, and anxiousness to one of being sourced by your natural intuitive "knowing," having your life held in the context of your eternal nature, living in the "now," sourced by your *Self*, and experiencing the world for what it is: a physical dimension in which to experience and bring forth living your best life and experiencing the peace and joy you were meant to in this lifetime.

## Paul, Business Owner

I know when it's my *Self* that is speaking because I'm very related to the distinct difference in the tone, vibration, and resonance of my *Self* versus my *Mind's* energy. How I tell the difference is because the language and experience of the communication of my *Self* sound so different than the *Mind*. My *Mind* sounds firm, strong, and hard. My *Self* is more relaxed, at ease, and peaceful. I Connect a lot around my family. So a specific time was when I was attending our family reunion. We have an annual family gathering for my side, and it always brings up my past relationships with my brothers and how I think they view me (from my *Mind* of course) and what happens during the time I spend with them. So this time happened to be a golf tournament, and I Connected about it before we went into the tournament. And what I got from my *Self* was to just completely be with them and don't get hooked by anything, just be there for the relationship and just enjoy it. I remember there were things that were said where I would get triggered, and it was stuff where they said things that would deliberately try to trigger me, like stuff about the game, or how I was playing, etc. I could feel my *Body* cringe inside, and then I would let it go and just be with them. And it was very interesting, because at

the end of the round of golf, my older brother acknowledged me for being so available, and so open, and it
shifted how I related to him and he related to me. For the
most part whenever I'm at any kind of family gathering,
there's always something that my *Mind* gets kicked up
about that I have to then know that there's a journey here
that I'm walking with them and that there's something in
it for me and something in it for them. So I always look to
my *Self* for what's in it for me inside of the unfolding of my
journey with them. And when I do that, it unquestionably
always moves toward another level of relatedness and
love in that relationship.

## A New Relationship to the Physical Realm

When you Connect, you are redefining the material
world, its role in your journey, and your view of the physical realm. You begin to access a different relationship to
the physical realm. From the *Mind* the physical realm *is*
your only journey. You go to the physical world for how to
feel, who you are, who you need to be and should be, what
is important to be happy and successful, what matters in
life, why you need to have and do things in your life. The
*Mind* is related to the physical realm as the only paradigm;
hence from the current paradigm we are energetically
related to the physical realm as our world and universe.

We know we will die one day, but the *Mind* lives like
this is way in the future and it processes this as a one
day someday, but not now. The *Mind* resonates with an
illusion that we'll keep going forever. We go to bed in the
energy that there is a tomorrow. The *Mind* disconnects
that we are energy.

### Gina, Social Media and Press Manager

The more I Connect, the more the phrase "all is well" really has come into existence for me, and that's huge for me. It has helped to shut my *Mind* up, and considering that I live in this very chaotic place, New York City, that's a huge difference for me. It gives me a sense of peace of mind. Philosophically I could always get that as a concept intellectually, but what this work has done is that it has allowed that to actually become a part of my life, not just a philosophy. To really get it and start to apply it are a big deal for me. It's not about attaining anything; it really is about being able to go about life peacefully and have it be more of a journey. It cuts down on a lot of stress.

When you begin to Connect, you shift how the physical world is occurring. You shift into an energy that the physical world is only one dimension of life. It is the opportunity to bring your *Self* to the world.

For humanity as a whole, this is a place for us to bring all of our *Self* and have it be experienced by each other from our *Self*. We can hold the universe and the planet and have our actions honor all of it. We can be with the trees, the animals, the land, and honor all of it. We can live in the vibration of what these elements are designed for—to give us the gift of an earth where we can honor all of the living energies, which will shape anew our experience of the journey. We can bring our Selves to how and what we express as an opportunity to share and contribute. We are led to bring the deepest part of our being to each other. We share, and in doing so, it allows for our oneness to be a catalyst for having all that we need to exist on the planet.

When we bring our Selves to the physical realm, we define the physical realm for what it is and how it is designed to support us in fulfilling our journey. The physical realm shifts from defining us to our having our Selves creating its rules and laws as a place where we each get to know and experience the joy of being our true Selves.

## A Redefining of the *Mind* as a Tool for Your Journey

The step of Connecting brings forth a redefining of the *Mind* as a tool for the journey of *Self*. The *Mind* is a mechanism that is designed to support our functioning as a human being. It is what joins us to all our actions. It provides the stimulus and the messages needed to have us function physically. It is the connector to our physical form—our *Body*.

Without this new paradigm, the *Mind* operates as our only paradigm, for it is what we listen, trust, and act from on a daily basis. It is where we automatically go for the answers to our questions. It immediately supplies us with the answers it thinks we need to handle situations. It is designed to ensure we are never threatened or destroyed, because it is designed to have us survive. It will destroy before we are destroyed. It will attack before we are attacked. It will protect and shut down our openness, our compassion, and our pure love whenever it perceives that we may not be the center of our universe. It strives to keep us in control of all situations, and it creates the perception that we must protect ourselves from all that the *Mind* has deciphered is threatening to us (as in the physical world). How often have you gotten so worked up over something that it seems like it's life or death, and afterward looked back on the situation and thought, "Why did I get so upset? That wasn't a big deal at all!" This is why we are so stressed out all the time. The *Mind* has *us* react to many non-life-threatening situations as life-threatening, keeping our *Body* in a fight or flight mode all the time.

When you Connect to your *Self*, you disconnect all of those *Mind* energies. You activate the energy of *Self*, of being Trusting and honoring the situation and each other. You are able to have your questions about life answered and are given actions to take, even when it is not what your *Mind* feels is right.

When you Connect, Listen, Trust, and Act, the *Mind* becomes a tool for what is now vibrating as your *Self*. Before Connecting, the *Mind* is who you are. When you Connect, you are saying and acknowledging that you are *not* your *Mind*, and therefore the whole context for the *Mind* shifts.

### The Practice of Connecting

Connecting is not meditation —it is unto itself an action that brings you into a moment of "now," allowing you to relate to your *Self* as real. To Connect *is* to acknowledge that when you honor your *Self* you are saying that you exist as your *Self*.

It is not dependent on anyone or anything else as a medium or a channel or a receptor for your access to your *Self*—Connecting is recognizing that you *are* your highest *Self now*. This is a profound shift in awareness and in our consciousness.

Imagine if everyone chose this as their truth and honored their *Self* as who they are now. Not relating to it as "one day when we are enlightened or when we have removed ourself from where we are, or when we have attained a new level of spiritual awakening—then we will experience the peace and joy of being our *Self*." Connecting occurs in a moment. Each moment of Connecting ignites and presences that truth as an energy—you are honoring your highest *Self* as you, "now."

In the beginning it takes time to develop your access to Connecting to your *Self*. To begin to Connect requires a place where it is quiet. Having a quiet place and closing your eyes are a start to shutting off the *Mind's* programming to see the physical world, which disengages your senses from being pulled into the physical dimension of life. The best and most effective way is to have a place in your home where you Connect. It is something to create. You are creating a new action in your life. This action is not in order to make anything happen—to use Connecting to fix your life or to Connect in order to have a great life . . . that would be the *Mind's* intention. You will have a great life when you Connect, Listen, Trust, and Act, because your *Self* will always unfold a great life. It may not look and feel like it from the *Mind*, but it is a great life because it is the one of your *Self*. So if you are here to be your *Self*, then having a place to Connect as a way of life is what there is to create in your physical realm so that Connecting can exist in your physical world.

Connecting requires that you disengage yourself from the *Mind's* physical connection to life. In the beginning this is what will develop your ability to Listen for the difference between your *Self's* energy and the energy of the *Mind*. At some point your access to Connecting will be as natural as listening to your *Mind* talking to you. You can make the switch from your *Mind* to your *Self* naturally and effortlessly anywhere anytime. It will be like flipping a switch. You will have brought yourself to living from your *Self* in your daily living as a human being.

## Connecting Step-by-Step

In the beginning when you Connect, you won't necessarily know the difference in the energy of your *Mind* versus your *Self*. As you write down what you get, you will develop a relationship to the words your *Mind* says, i.e., "should," "want," "have to," and any strong views of the situation.

As you live this as a way of life, you will soon have an awareness of the difference in energy, and at any time you can disconnect the *Mind* to seek into what is resonating from your *Self*.

As you will see in the Act chapter, it is only when your Actions are coming from your *Self* that you shift your life into the vibration and resonance of a new paradigm where your *Self* is the dominant energy that your life is organized around. It is here that all unfolds naturally and effortlessly.

Close your eyes. Envision yourself unplugging the Mind, releasing its energy and vibration. Imagine all of your worries and concerns floating away from you in tiny little bubbles.

Continue to release all of the *Mind's* truths about you, your life, and the physical world. This allows you to experience yourself as separate from your *Mind*.

Keep taking deep breaths as you surrender into your *Self* by releasing the *Mind* and unplugging all of the *Mind's* truths. The act of releasing the *Mind* is a state change in your vibrational resonance.

Begin to presence your *Self* as energy. Starting from the top of your head, ignite your cells with the vibration and resonance of your higher *Self*. By simply opening to this awareness, you are activating the frequency in alignment with your highest and truest *Self*.

Be with each cell awakening with the vibration of itself as an eternal energy. The energy that is resonating in each cell is that of your eternal *Self*. Presence your DNA vibrating as your "inner knowing" is now activated as You.

Allow yourself to experience this energy vibrating and resonating within you as You. Feel the vibration throughout your *Body*. Be with this energy as real with the "knowing" that this is the You of your highest *Self*. Allow yourself to Connect to this energy as a real life force of consciousness evoking and emitting your *Self*.

Notice the *Mind* energy as directing, telling, "knowing," necessary, right, strong, determined, clear, logical, important, only interested in its point of view of what is happening. Give yourself a lot of room to experience the *Mind* for its own unique design and role. Begin to create your relationship to your *Mind* as one of having a *Mind* but knowing that it is simply the *Mind*—a tool for you to know your *Self*, a necessary dimension of you to unfold your highest *Self* this lifetime.

Notice the energy of your *Self*—an opposite vibration from the *Mind*. It is always soft, loving, caring, assuring, affirming of "all is well," an evoking of deep love and compassion, an "inner knowing" of divine truth, an energetic shift cellularly, Connected to a oneness, a shift in awareness of energy as real, an inner awareness of *Self* as real, peace, ease, grace, an engulfing feeling that "you are whole."

Practice disconnecting the *Mind's* thoughts to allow your *Self* to resonate. In making the choice to know that you are not your *Mind*, begin to experience a powerful Connection to your *Self*. Bring your awareness to the *Mind's* constant monologue occurring in your thoughts. Begin to see it as the *Mind*. You are simply choosing to have no interest in anything the *Mind* is saying. You are bringing forth your *Self* as who you will now Listen, Trust, and Act from.

Ask your *Self* questions and get answers to questions that are unique to you. Connect to the question: "What is there for me to know about _____?" and then presence any area/situation/circumstance that you want to get answers from your *Self* about.

The question, "What is there for me to know?" is a state change in how you are resonating—for you are saying, "I know that my *Self* is my reality and I am only interested in what is there to know from my *Self* about this area of my life." You are continuously activating the vibration of your *Self* as real as you disconnect the *Mind* to bring forth your truth of who you are in that moment by presencing, "What is there for me to know?"

This statement *is* the *only* access to a new paradigm—you are disconnecting all of the *Mind's* truth as your paradigm to embrace and honor the paradigm of You as your *Self*.

- Now presence and evoke the question, "What actions am I to be in around this area?" You are stating and affirming a new truth that what there is to act on from your *Self* is what you are here to honor. You are further presencing that when your actions are shaped from your *Self*, what will unfold in that area will only and always honor your highest truth and the highest expression of what there is to unfold in that area.

- Be sure to write down whatever is being evoked from your *Self*. It is important to immediately write down what is there when you Connect. It takes a few short minutes, in some cases just seconds, before the *Mind* is once again shaping, driving, and presencing what is occurring. As such it is important and necessary to write down what was experienced, felt, evoked, or heard during the Connection around both statements. This allows you to develop, in how you Listen, the difference between the energies of your *Mind* distinct from the energies of your *Self*.

(To hear an mp3 audio that will walk you through the exercise of Connecting, go to www.indiratoday.com/connect/self.)

## How Connecting Alters Your Life

The step of Connecting is the beginning of shifting you into the vibration of your true *Self*. It is only when you can disconnect the *Mind* and Connect to your *Self* that you activate a new paradigm and as such create an energetic shift in how you view life and everything around you. As you experience living from the vibration of your *Self*, you will experience a shift in how you experience life when you are acting from your *Mind* distinct from your *Self*. You will bring a new awareness to living life as your *Self* as your only reality. Living from the vibration of your true *Self* evokes the joy that life is designed for each of us to experience as human beings.

Connecting is the step to activating in your DNA the truth that you are an eternal being as energy. This shift is a new reality and a new paradigm. We hold this as a conversation, separate and distinct from the *Mind's* knowing of life, giving us access to living this reality as our truth.

This shift in energy and vibration releases a force of energy that aligns a new frequency within your DNA. Your cells become aligned with this new truth. This force of energy is now activated to align and bring forth all that can be known as an eternal being. You are open to the vortex of energy/vibration that houses all truths and allows you to know your divine *Self*.

This is a new paradigm. It does exist, and it is now available to all of us, for we are all designed to be our True and Highest *Self*.

A powerful event occurs in the moment of Connecting. You disconnect the *Mind's* truth as your reality. Nothing can compare to a human being experiencing the disconnection of their *Mind's* truth as their reality. The *Mind* is designed to never disconnect from our current paradigm. In the step of Connecting it is a state change in a frequency where the paradigm of the *Mind* is in the background and the vibration of our *Self* flows to the forefront. We shift into a new paradigm that has us operate in the realm we were designed to experience as our *Self* and life.

The *Mind's* paradigm is no longer what vibrates as your truth. It is a momentous moment of "now." It is why Connecting as a way of life is the pathway to living a new paradigm.

The activating and arising of the energy called your *Self* as who you are is *all* there is for you to do to have your life unfold with the ease and natural flow of your highest intentions.

This could seem foreign to the *Mind*—nothing to do; that is impossible. But note that you *are* doing something—you are claiming a new truth that your *Self* is already here for a journey to experience itself and that by simply presencing "What is there for me now?" and "What actions am I to be in?" you are activating as energy a new truth that life is effortless and that our best life arises as we simply take the actions we get to take from *Self*. This is all we came here for, to know our *Self* as we have our actions align with the journey of our *Self*.

How do you know that that is happening? By Connecting to what Actions to be in and taking those Actions in the physical realm.

When you Connect, Listen, Trust, and Act as a way of life, you align yourself with the vibration and resonance of the "Universal Consciousness." Imagine that You, as *Self*, chose a physical form to experience your *Self*. Your *Self* is eternal and vibrates in a frequency with your divine nature. So, as you have your Actions, at any time, come from your *Self*, you are activating the Universal alignment that is naturally there for you to live and be your best *Self*.

In living your life from Connecting to your *Self* for everything there is to know and Act on, you will begin to experience the divine nature of You. This happens naturally. This journey is embedded in your DNA, it is who you are. It is the simplicity of life. To Act from your *Self* through Connecting is to be in Universal alignment.

As you live a life where your actions are organized around a new awareness of knowing that you are Acting from your *Self* not your *Mind*, there arises an ease and a joy that unfolds and manifests what the Universe, the God-consciousness, is here to unfold as your birthright. You experience life as a journey where "all is well" and "all is as it should be" are the new context for living life.

## ≈ 5 ≈

# Listen: Claiming a New Paradigm
# of YOU as Energy

The step of Listening is acknowledging that you are energy. When you Listen, you are paying attention to the You that is the eternal vibration of Energy. You are beginning to relate to yourself not as a *Body* and a *Mind* but rather a force of divine energy that chose to be here in a physical form.

In the step of Listening you are bringing forth and having your Actions align with what your *Self* is saying is real. The *Mind* is not saying this is real, your *Self* is. In order to first acknowledge that you are not your *Mind*, your *Self* has to show up.

Who is it that is acknowledging that you are not your *Mind*—not the *Mind*, of course—therefore, for that simple statement to have a profound effect, you begin to know that there is a You that is separate from the *Mind*. The step of Listening defines the truth that what is real is the energy of your *Self*. It brings the new paradigm into existence as a reality. It brings the duality into existence as a dimension of your journey here on earth. In the energy of Listening you are embracing energy as a dimension of you that you are honoring. You are redefining who you are. You are redirecting the *Mind* into a new paradigm. You are presencing the statement: "I am energy."

In doing so the *Mind* begins to embrace that as a part of its paradigm. When the *Mind* gets that the *Self* is real, it begins to allow the dimension of energy to resonate and vibrate as real. You begin to bring a new paradigm into your life.

The step of Listening deepens the truth that your *Self* is who you are and why you are here. The act of Listening is you giving honor to your *Self*. What is it you are listening to? The energy and resonance of your *Self*. You are listening to your *Self* because you are saying that Connecting and Listening to your *Self* are living your life from why you came and what you are here for. You are aligning your life with your authentic *Self*. You are acknowledging that your *Self* is YOU.

## Developing Your Power to Listen

Just like Connecting, Listening is an active process. It is not arbitrary or casual. You do not find yourself Connecting or Listening by accident. You are choosing to bring into your life a different "knowing"—that you are not your *Mind* and that your *Self* is who you are.

In this context the step of Listening shifts how you relate to the *Mind*. The *Mind* becomes a tool. It becomes a very powerful and necessary tool to exist in your *Body* and to unfold and fulfill the journey of your *Self*. In the step of Listening, you create a new relationship to your *Mind* as a tool from which you can unfold and live your highest and best *Self*.

In this step you activate a deeper resonance and vibration of the "knowing" of your *Self* as You. You shift energetically from how you vibrate as the *Mind*, to now activating the vibration of your *Self* as real.

The "knowing" that you are not your *Body* or *Mind* is not something to work through the *Mind*. That is in the current paradigm. When you shift your energetic resonance through Connecting and Listening, you are shifting how your cells vibrate. In doing so you activate your "inner knowing" of who you are as real.

You naturally have your *Body* and your *Mind* be tools for your journey. The new paradigm of energy is now a dimension that is real and tangible. Your *Mind* shifts how it resonates in that moment, and your *Body* becomes an energy from which you can Connect for all that you need to know to honor it.

### Todd, Chief Strategy Officer

The first time I Connected to my *Self*, I could clearly distinguish between the feeling of my *Body* energy, and there was another energy that I could distinguish as my *Mind*, and it was after being aware of those two energies that I was able to feel something else. It was very distinct, and when I Listened, there was a dialog available there. It was a vibration and resonance, and I knew it was my *Self*. The more I've been Connecting, the more distinct that feeling of Listening to my *Self* is. It's like a physical vibration and energy that are there. The words that come to me from *Self* are different than those that my *Mind* would generate. It's almost like there's a different copywriter sending

*(continued)*

me the copy. It's more genuine when it's coming from my *Self*. Even my interactions with my business partner and my employees are more genuine when I Listen to my *Self* rather than when I am coming from my *Mind*. It sets up a different way of interacting. When my *Mind* is kicked up about something, the first thing I do is become fiercely aware of my *Body's* energy. So I might tap my knee and become keenly aware of that. And then I heighten the awareness of my *Mind's* energy. So I really hyper-heighten the awareness of both of these energies, *Body* first, and then *Mind*. I become so aware of them that then I can just drop both. And then I can just ask a question and let both of them drop and all of a sudden the *Self* energy is able to emerge, and I can isolate the feeling of the vibration of this empty and calm place where the communication is different to be able to Listen to my *Self*.

In the new paradigm, honoring your *Body* is a natural flow from Connecting, Listening, Trusting, and Acting. The vibrational shift in how you resonate has you tend to honoring your *Body* as an access to your journey. Without a *Body*, you don't have a journey. In the new paradigm this is an energy that is strong.

## Living in an Awareness That This Journey Is a Duality

In the step of Listening you are forging the duality. You are Listening for the energy of your *Self*, as a distinct energy from your *Mind*. You are developing your natural ability to hear your *Self* as effortlessly as you hear your *Mind*. You are bringing this paradigm into existence as a new paradigm from which to live your life.

The separation of the *Mind's* energy from the energy of your *Self*—the tone, vibration, and resonance—is a new paradigm. The new paradigm embraces the duality as a dimension of life.

The *Mind* will always be claiming control in your daily life. So you embrace that as a part of who you are, knowing that the duality is the access to living from your *Self*. The embracing of the *Mind*, as real, allows for more access to your *Self*. This is not about one or the other. This is about knowing what role each plays and empowering that role.

Listening is the step that activates a vibration of knowing that your inner *Self* is a "radio station" that is always on—and when you Listen, you are tuning into the "radio station." In the current paradigm, this does not exist. In the new paradigm, the "radio station" becomes clear and available anytime as you develop your ability to Listen to your inner *Self* for what there is to know at any time about anything.

You Listen because you are acknowledging this "inner knowing" as you. You are acknowledging that, at conception, You fused with a *Mind* and a *Body* to be in this journey, and this journey is marvelous. It is remarkable. But the only way to live this journey is to have it exist as a different paradigm than the paradigm of the *Mind*.

In Listening you make the leap, you are in the Connection, you are with You. You are being you, honoring you, developing a Connection to your "inner knowing" as who you are.

The step of Listening is you honoring You. You are actively having the *Mind* embrace You as your *Self*. You are saying that the You of your *Self* is You. You are claiming the "knowing" of your eternal vibration. You are redefining the "knowing" of what is real as your *Self*. You are presencing that the energy of *Self* is real and is You. A contextual shift arises as a new truth; a new frequency resonates and vibrates as your reality as you Listen to the energy of You as You, for its truth.

## What Is Being Evoked in Listening

The energy that is being evoked as real in Listening is that your *Self* chose once again to be in a physical form to experience itself. In the step of Listening you are activating a vibration of your *Self* on its journey. You are activating your *Self* as your reality. The step of Listening is presencing a new vibration that you are eternal, you are here as a divine presence, and you are here to live this You.

In Listening you are tuning into the "radio station" of your *Self*. You are paying attention to the tone vibration and resonance of *Self*. The tone resonance and vibration of *Self* is soft, it is always "all is well," loving, never a right or wrong, never a good or bad, never about a result, never about anything related to fulfilling or accomplishing something in the physical plane.

The energy of *Self* is only in the eternal nature of our vibration. It vibrates in a "knowing" that we may or may not be in a *Body*. It resonates with a nonattachment to anything physical, such as money, things, or what the *Mind* says it needs—if you find yourself listening for answers such as these, you are in the *Mind*. If you find yourself listening to make more money, you are in the *Mind*. If you are listening for something to get better, or for you to be happier, you are in the *Mind*.

The energy of *Self* is only about what is there in our behavior that will transcend our *Mind* to have our Actions evoke our honoring of our *Self* and each other.

In the step of Listening there is a vibrational shift in how you resonate. Your cells, your DNA begin to vibrate and resonate in alignment with the frequency and vibration of your highest *Self*. You find yourself bringing forth more of how to interact and Connect to your *Self* as a natural way of living your life. In the new paradigm, life is not about the struggle and effort of making something happen—it is the shift in how you resonate as Connecting and Listening become a way of living life.

In the step Listening your DNA and your cells are being activated in a new and distinct vibration for what is real from your eternal *Self*. You begin to resonate in a vibration that has your natural and intuitive "knowing" be what you honor as your *Self*.

You find yourself Listening and relating to life from a new energy that shapes your Actions in alignment with how your *Self* would be in a "now." Life becomes less about the future or a destination, and life becomes full of an experience of being in the "now," knowing that you are eternal and all is well. These new truths become a new energy from which you hold and see life.

## Opening Up a New Paradigm for What Is Possible in Your Life

In this new energy, you are opening up a new paradigm for what is possible in your life. You begin to slow life down. You begin to smell the roses naturally. You begin to honor each moment of "now." This is all occurring from a shift in how you resonate and vibrate. This is not something to do or to fix, and it is not about trying to change the *Mind's* views and thoughts. This is evoking a Listening of your *Self* as You.

The step of Listening is to begin to relate to your *Self* as energy. You begin to Listen to the energy of your *Self* as You, and in Listening you begin to evoke and presence the vibration and the tone and the resonance of this energy as real. In Listening you access the speaking of your eternal *Self*. This *Self* is communicating what there is for you to know about what is occurring in the "now" of your journey.

All of what is occurring is directly related to the journey You chose to experience. To know what there is about the journey from your *Self* is where Listening becomes an access to the new paradigm of having your *Self* be what you Trust and Act on.

You begin to relate to the resonance of energy from the words you are hearing. You begin to match the words you are hearing with the tone and vibration and frequency of the energy—you begin to develop the "knowing" of your *Mind's* energy distinct from the energy of your *Self*. Energy vibrates and resonates in the frequency of the "knowing" of your highest *Self*. As you develop your awareness of relating to energy as real, you begin to allow yourself to be with the vibration and resonance such that language arises.

This is the experience of living from a new paradigm. It is a paradigm where your actions come from your "inner knowing." You begin to live from a new paradigm that energy is real, and you can Connect to the energy of your *Self* for the words that are being spoken as your *Self*. Just as the *Mind* is speaking words so is your *Self*.

You begin to have a relationship to the energy of your *Self* for how it vibrates, such that the language of your *Self* is available to you as naturally as your *Mind's* language.

As you begin a life of Connecting and Listening, you develop your ability to know your *Mind* separate from your *Self*. You begin to have a natural access to the duality of both, choosing to Listen to your *Self* for what is being communicated. It is the ability to tell the difference between your *Mind* and your *Self* that gives you more access to your *Self*. This is developed in your Listening. You begin to bring a Listening to the energy of each as a separate and distinct energy.

## Maria, Natural Health Coach, Yoga Teacher

For me, Listening to my *Self* is a quieter experience than my normal waking busy experience of the *Mind*. I go into my heart center, and it's a feeling of disconnecting my *Mind* for sure, and being in a higher vibration. The answers I get from my *Self* are very different, especially about my relationships with people. My *Mind* often has very big judgments and opinions about people. My *Mind* is very active, and very busy, and very fast. I'm really capable in business, so my *Mind* is almost addicted to the adrenaline rush of being so competent, capable, confident, and "better-than" in business. It becomes superior sometimes, and from my *Mind*, that's more important than relationships. The task at hand becomes too important. For example, when I first started Connecting, I was just getting out of the mortgage brokerage business, and I would often Connect about things like, "What am I going to do now to make money?" and I would get messages from my *Self* like, "Go for a walk on the beach," or "Go have lunch with your mother." I remember getting really annoyed about it.

*(continued)*

I was like "Really? How is going to lunch with my mom going to help with that?" I think the journey from my *Self* at that time was really to have me reconnect with my relationships, because I had so shut them off, like the only thing that was important to me was surviving in the material world, and being successful in business and making money. When I Connect and Listen to my *Self*, I get much more loving and compassionate answers about life. Those answers seem more soothing and comforting in my life.

## Being in a "Now" Identifying Your *Mind's* Mechanism

The step of Listening activates you to be in a "now." As you Listen, you are making the switch from the current paradigm of time and linearity to presencing an awareness of energy as eternal and real. In that moment there is no Mind—there is no past or future—there is simply the moment of "now," whereby you are choosing to hear the language of your *Self* as You.

In this moment, in the step of Listening, you are continuously releasing the Mind, allowing you to Listen for the energy and vibration of your *Self*. In the step of Listening, you are dealing with the Mind as a separate and distinct energy from your *Self*. You are seeing and identifying the Mind at play, and as you release the Mind's mechanism, you begin to activate your *Self* and hear your *Self*.

This is all occurring in the realm of energy. You are relating to Mind and *Self* as energy, and you are Listening for what there is from your *Self*, for what there is for you to know about whatever is occurring for you in life.

Each of you has a very distinct *Mind*. Each person's *Mind* is designed to operate from the patterns that keep your *Self* removed for your consciousness. As you learn to bring language to your *Mind*, you begin to have more access to your *Self*. The following is a guide to beginning to bring language to your *Mind*.

1. Pick a situation where you got annoyed, upset, or concerned. Write down all of what the *Mind* is saying. If your *Mind* swears . . . write that down. Write more than just the story; include your opinion and your points of view about the situation and the other person or people in the situation.

2. Read it out loud to yourself and listen to the strong, hard words and sentences which came from your *Mind*.

3. Highlight the phrases you have said before in other situations.

4. Note to yourself that all of what you wrote is your *Mind* not You.

The only way to get access to Listening to the difference between *Mind* and *Self* is through the act of Connecting. Without Connecting, the *Mind* will begin to take the exercise of *Mind* and *Self* and now operate from the current paradigm. It is only in the step of Connecting that you have an energetic shift in how you are vibrating and resonating, such that the step of Listening is now available to you as a pathway to Trust and Act.

In Listening you are only interested in what your *Self* is communicating. You are Listening for *Self*, for what there is for you to know from *Self*. You are acknowledging your *Self* as You, and you are Trusting and Acting from what is being evoked and communicated from your *Self* as what there is to honor.

You develop a natural way of living life, where you are interested in Listening to your *Self* in as many areas of your life as possible. Experiencing a new paradigm is a direct correlation to how much you are Listening for what there is from *Self* to know and Trust and Act on in your life. Knowing that you are only interested in what your *Self* is communicating is a new paradigm, for it reshapes how the *Mind* begins to operate as tool for the journey.

## A Pathway to Your Best Life

Developing a Connection to your *Self* where you know that it is You will unquestionably guide you to your best life. This will only shift as your life begins to have more and more of your actions come from your *Self*. It is impossible to hold this conversation from the *Mind*, because for the *Mind*, there is only the logic and the need to understand—that is the way of the *Mind*.

It is only when you embrace Connecting, Listening, Trusting, and Acting as a pathway to living your life from the paradigm of your *Self*—because you acknowledge that you are *not* your *Mind*—that you begin to shift the energy, vibration, and frequency in which you resonate. In this shift, the energetic realm in which you exist alters. Your energetic vibration is aligning itself with the You of your highest *Self*. Life shifts around you. Your speaking shifts, your views shift, what is important and necessary for you shifts. This is what is now here as your life.

In the step of Listening you begin to develop more and more prowess in seeing the Mind's play in all of your life and what is happening. You begin to want to know your Self's communication such that you can Trust and Act from your Self. In this journey you become organized around this: to listen for what is coming from the Mind and what is coming from the Self as a way of living. In its simplest form, that is your journey.

To live from your Self as you transcend the Mind allows you to experience life as the journey you chose. The life you came to know and experience becomes your life. The life of your Self becomes your life. You begin to shift to your Self and you begin to live in the duality.

You find yourself willing to Trust and Act on things that are foreign to your Mind, not of any interest to your Mind, but clearly a communication from your Self to Trust and Act on—you experience life as the journey You chose, and it feels different. You are bringing You to all of the world.

## The Physical Realm Becomes the Access to Experience You

In the step of Listening you are presencing the physical realm as the access to experiencing your Self. In the step of Listening you are always open to hearing the answer to "What actions am I to be in?"

The Mind always knows what actions there are for you to be in, so without Connecting to your Self to Listen for "What actions am I to be in?" your actions are coming from the conclusions and the patterns of what your Mind thinks your life should be about. Do you think the *Mind* of someone that killed somebody is coming from that person's *Self*? Do you think the child abuser's behavior is coming from their *Self*? Do you think the sly moves of a thief are coming from their *Self*? Of course not, these are all actions that came from the *Mind's* energy, not the *Self*.

In the step of Listening, you are always Connecting to and Listening for "What actions am I to be in?" for it is *only* in taking the actions from your *Self* that you will live in a new paradigm. This is where the physical realm becomes an access to experiencing your *Self*: the *Self* of love, of understanding, of compassion, of transcending the *Mind's* energy of separation and creating others as better than or unequal or wrong because of their color or religion, etc. It is here in the physical plane that you get to play out being your highest *Self*. This is the life you want to live. This is the life you came to live.

In the step of Listening, you are making a shift from the *Mind's* paradigm to the paradigm of your *Self*. You eliminate fear, concern, and worry as way of life no matter the circumstances. From the paradigm of *Self* there is *no* fear, worry, or concern. All is as it needs to be when you are in the energy of *Self*. In the energy of *Self* there are no "shoulds," no "have-tos," no right or wrong, no good or bad, nothing that shouldn't be—it is *all* the journey you have set up to experience. This puts whatever is occurring in your hands. You become the source of all that is happening around you and to you. You get to Connect and Listen for what there is to know about what is happening. It is when you are only going to the *Mind* for what there is to know that you are present to fear, anxiety, concern, and worry. All that is there in the eternal vibration is the resonance that is vibrating as You.

## You Begin to View Life through a New Pair of Lenses—Those of Your Eternal *Self*

In the step of Listening you begin to develop a view of life from the lens of your *Self*. The physical things around you begin to have a place in relationship to your journey. Where you live, what your needs are, what you want to have, all start to come from your *Self*. In other words, if at any moment we may not be in our *Body*, then all of what is happening is only for the experience of our *Self*, not the things that the *Mind* has an attachment to. Therefore, if each moment of "now" is a new moment from which to activate the vibration of our "knowing" of who we are, then in each moment we can make choices about what action best serves our *Self*, which is the honoring of our *Self* and each other. This becomes the driver of our life. Imagine a life lived from that paradigm.

From the step of Listening there is even an energetic shift in how money occurs and vibrates. From the current paradigm the energy of money vibrates strongly. Money is the energy that dominates. From the new paradigm money is a tool for the journey of our *Self*. Money is the tool to allow us to function and be here to experience our *Self*. Interestingly, when you are living in the new para-digm, having money is not the focus. Your focus becomes about your journey, which unfolds through Connecting, Listening, Trusting, and Acting.

As your Actions in life come from your *Self*, you find yourself going through your journey with money shifting from the *Mind's* view of it to how your *Self* resonates. In this process, you find yourself having what is needed for you to be here, and whether you have a lot or a little is no longer the question—the question becomes "Are your actions aligned with the journey of your *Self*?" For when your journey is aligned with your *Self*, money is there as a part of your journey—a little or a lot becomes a matter of the *Mind's* view, nothing to do with your *Self*.

You live in a state of peace knowing you are fulfilling what you came here to experience. In the step of Listening, you develop a powerful relationship to the duality and know that you are here to only honor your *Self* because it is You. In this energy you are at peace. You are not wondering what the right thing is or what you should be doing. You are not within the *Mind's* need to leap ahead and figure life out, or to plan ahead to set goals and objectives. I am not saying don't do those things, but what you get through Connecting and Listening becomes the pathway that naturally shapes your life. You experience being in your purpose. I define purpose as to have your actions in each moment of "now" come from your *Self*, distinct from your *Mind*.

As you live this way, you begin to live in a new paradigm of your eternal nature. You begin to experience life for why and how it was designed to be—a gift for the journey of your spirit, your highest *Self*. You house in your being the "knowing" of your *Self* as real. You can hold the physical world as a place where you are here for this moment of "now" and know that it is a journey, and this moment is a moment to honor. No longer do you need difficult times or tragic situations to jolt you into that paradigm; you bring that naturally as you live each day in the "now" honoring your *Self*.

Life is now organized around seeing the *Mind*, and transcending it, to Listen to your *Self*. You are in life to bring forth Listening to your *Self* for what there is to know and for what actions there are for you to be in. This state change produces a shift in awareness and consciousness. You begin to open up to your *Self* as a strong and natural channel that is on and can be Listened for in your daily life. You begin to be able to tell when the *Mind* is running life and to shift to your *Self* where you are Listening for what actions to be in. You find yourself in the joy and ease of life, knowing that all is well. Life will unfold in highest and best journey.

# ⊚ 6 ⊚

# Trust: Activating Your "Inner Knowing" of *Self* as YOU

Once you have Connected and Listened for what your *Self* is letting you know, the next important step is to TRUST what you have received. Trust what you have gotten to be in action about, no matter what your *Mind* says about it. Sometimes the message you hear defies the logic of the *Mind*. Our relationship to life from the *Mind* is linear and logical. From energy, the universe is not linear. You could say, from energy, the universe operates through a purposeful chaotic unfolding, because everything is in a relationship with everything else. So, when one piece moves, it changes the entire relationship with everything else. When this happens, what can happen next *changes* because the energy of everything has shifted, allowing for a new relationship and a new result. The Trust step is going deeper into your "inner knowing" of *Self*. It is activating your "inner knowing" as who you are, not from a thought or a concept, but as a reality. You are Trusting what you are getting from your *Self*. You are Listening to your *Self* as You.

You have released the *Mind* as your truth to heed the truth of your *Self* as real. You have brought into the physical realm the speaking of your *Self*, the "inner knowing" that is the blueprint of your best life.

## Paul, CEO of a Consulting Firm

I remember a time when we were working really hard to generate some new business. I Connected on a Monday to see what there was for me to know from my *Self* about expanding and opening up new business. What I got was, "Go to the gym!" This made no sense. In fact, I thought I must have heard it wrong. So I Connected again and got the same message. My *Mind* was arguing for, "Just go to work." One of the things I realized awhile ago is to just *trust* what I get. So, Monday through Thursday I *went* to the gym. On Thursday afternoon, I got a call from an executive about doing some work in his company. He said he was referred to me by one of my clients from the past. This opened up a major piece of new business for us. Since then I do not question anything I get from my Connections, I simply Trust what I get.

In the step of Trusting you begin to see life through the eyes of your *Self* from what you are getting in your Connections. You are Listening to your *Self* for what there is to know, and you are honoring this by Trusting what is being said. You are surrendering to your *Self* as You, and you are beginning to integrate its vibration and its communication as You. In the step of Trusting you are releasing ALL of the *Mind's* views and reality, to embrace this new paradigm of your *Self*. You begin to embrace this communication as what you will give your life to—you begin to hear this communication as what you will honor and Trust as your life. You bring yourself to a new frequency and resonance that the communication from your *Self* as what you are living from now.

Trust is a state change in how you are vibrating. You embody the resonance and vibration of your highest *Self*. You become someone who has transcended that the physical realm is the only thing that is real to having your true and divine *Self* be who you are now. You have organized your cells around a new truth that who you are is your *Self*. You have activated a duality of *Mind* and *Self* as distinct and separate dimensions of You. You have brought forth the vibration of your *Self* as who you are with the *Mind* being designed as a tool for your journey.

In Trust there is a total release of the *Mind*. You have shifted the energies of the *Mind* as the only reality that your actions come from to having access to your *Self* in a duality. All of the *Mind's* truths and design are not resonating in the moment of "now" when you access your *Self*. You have created a vortex of bringing the energy of your eternal *Self* forth as the journey you are here to unfold. You are Trusting—you are saying—I am this Me, the Me of my eternal divine *Self*. You are Trusting that this You is what is real. You have claimed the You that fused with a *Body* and a *Mind*. You are powerfully connected to the totality of your *Self*.

The *Mind* is only a dimension of you. The energy that is now here transcends the physical realm of what and how the *Mind* works. The *Mind's* limitations, its truths that keep us disconnected from our *Self*, have been released. All of what cannot occur in the physical realm, from the *Mind*, is possible. You have activated a dimension of you that transcends the physical dimension. You have activated a vortex of vibration and energy, a force of consciousness that is not limited by the *Mind*. This is the journey of your *Self*.

## Developing Your Power to Trust

When you trust what you get after Connecting to your *Self*, you are developing your power to Trust, which in turn gives you more access to your *Self*. In developing your power to Trust, your relationship to the physical realm shifts as only part of the duality at play. As you activate this frequency and resonance of Trust, you begin to create for yourself a reality where the physical realm is included but is not the totality of who you are. You begin to have access to having the physical realm as a dimension of your journey while "knowing" that it is not related to your *Self*.

You develop the muscle of Trusting that your "inner knowing" is the reliable and best source to go to for all that you need to know about your life's journey. The physical realm becomes the playground for your *Self* to experience itself. You begin to operate in an energetic vibration that resonates with a new truth that your *Body* and your *Mind* are the tools you have to be in the physical plane. There is a shift in how you vibrate on the physical plane. The *Mind* begins to disconnect from truths that shape your daily, weekly, and monthly existence.

You begin to experience the energy of something first. Energy becomes real in your living of life. You experience the energy of what is occurring as your journey. You begin to develop a muscle in knowing the vibration and resonance of the energy of your *Self* as it unfolds in your life. You become at home with knowing your *Self* as energy. You experience a shift from knowing yourself as your *Body* to knowing yourself as energy. You begin to Listen to and Trust the energy of what is resonating about you, others, and life, and you vibrate with a "knowing" whether it is your *Mind* or your *Self*.

You become Connected to your *Self* as an eternal energy. This new paradigm becomes equally as real as the current paradigm. You can hold the energy of your eternal vibration as the real you. You experience a dimension of you that evokes a peace in "knowing" that you are in the world, but not of the world. You begin to trust your *Self* and honor this You. You begin to relate to the energy of your *Self* as the journey you came here to experience. Each moment of now becomes a gift in which to know your *Self* as real. You begin to see Connecting, Listening, Trusting, and Acting as the pathway to living your best and highest life. You seek into the relationships around you as an access to the journey to bring forth the reality of your true *Self*.

You now have access to a depth of "knowing" where the reality you perceive from your *Mind* is no longer your truth. You reshape and redefine your truth to be one that has access beyond what the *Mind's* limitations can ever know and experience.

## You Live in an Awareness of the "Now" as a Way of Living

All that exists is the "now." You are related to and connected to the "now" of the eternal divine energy called You. In the "now," all is available, all is possible, and all is "as it needs to be"—there is nothing that should be any different. Everything that is, is exactly as it needs to be for you to continue to unfold your divine *Self*. This is a profound and powerful moment, for in a moment of "now," you have transcended the *Mind's* relationship to what is occurring. This allows you to be void of the past and the future as a truth. It allows for a presencing of what is there as the truth from your *Self*.

It is here that you begin to elevate your vibration, how you resonate energetically. You are altering your cells, your DNA. You are transcending "karmic energies." You are aligning yourself with the "knowing" that in your eternal journey all that is occurring is what there is for you to experience to bring forth your highest *Self*.

Being in a "now" for more moments of life is a shifting from the current paradigm to experiencing a new paradigm of who you are and why you are here. This occurs as you Trust and then Act on what there is in each moment of "now" as your *Self*.

In the step of Trusting you become a force of energy on your eternal journey. You realign with your *Self*. You have become one with your *Self*—the *Self* that chose the journey to be in a *Body* and experience this lifetime. You have available to you all that has ever occurred for you in the times you have been in a physical form. You have available to you all of the experiences you have ever had since your beginning. This force of energy is the "Universal Consciousness" that aligns you with your very existence. You transcend all of the physical energies of earth as your reality to claim the vibration of your *Self* for what it knows and experiences at its core. This force begins to shape a new paradigm as the *Mind* embraces this as a dimension of you.

## You Experience the *Mind* as a Tool for You

It is in the step of Trusting that you alter the *Mind's* role in your journey as a human being. As you claim your *Self* as You, you are claiming the *Mind* as a tool for the journey of your *Self*. You are saying that you are relating to your *Self* as what you are here to honor. The energy of the *Mind* shifts how it vibrates in that moment. It is no longer the frequency that resonates in the current paradigm as real. It alters its role in how you experience your *Self* and your life. It shifts what the situations and circumstances around you are designed for. It shifts the view of your life from your *Mind* to your *Self*. The *Mind* is now in a new role of being in service to your *Self*. This is monumental.

You are in touch with the energy vibrating within you as You. You shift from being related to the world outside of you from what the *Mind* wants to the world within you that is organized around your journey and impact in life. You experience the energetic flow of vibration within you as a universe of consciousness that is more real than the physical world. Energy is your *only* reality. You are in the bliss and joy of knowing your *Self*. This energetic force is pulsating and resonating with the essence of the eternal You. You are swept into a vortex of deep "knowing" where you are at peace, all is well, all is as it needs to be, and there is nothing to fear—it is as you set it up to be—there is nothing outside of you to fear. From within, all will unfold powerfully for you to be your highest *Self*.

In this step you experience yourself as a part of the whole consciousness of the "Universal Vibration." There is no separation. You are one with all. You presence and activate a vibration where your connection to your *Self* houses all of life. It is a moment where you become one with All that there is, with the divine nature of yourself, with the God-essence that dwells as our true *Self*. You transcend the *Mind's* reality that you are separate and disconnected. You embrace your connection to all that is here; you transcend energies that keep you alone and isolated. You activate a new vibration that is a different You from the you of your *Mind*.

## The Knowing of Your *Self* Resonates More Loudly Than the *Mind*

In this step you are disconnected from fears, concerns, worry—for these only exist within the *Mind*. From your *Self* there is only what there is to know about the journey that is now unfolding. This is only accessible in a moment of "now." Outside of the "now," the *Mind* is calculating, projecting, deciding what is really happening—bringing your emotions to what the *Mind* has determined is what is happening. This has an impact on your physical and mental well-being. In the step of Trusting all that disappears. You are in the glory of "knowing" that you are here to shift all that is occurring from your *Mind's* view to the "knowing" of your *Self*. Your Self will *only* ever honor you, the people in your life and life itself. In the honoring you release and transcend the fears of the *Mind*. You become someone who is Trusting your *Self* not your *Mind*. You are redesigning yourself to live in a new paradigm of your *Self* as your true *Self*. You know that your *Self* is where to go for what there is to know about all and everything. It is a "radio station" that is on *all the time*. You know that living the road map of your *Self* will have you be the *Self* that is here to claim the world as You. You begin to know your magnificence in each moment of "now" that you Trust and Act from your *Self*. You become someone that is in the world, but not of the world.

You become someone that is at peace wherever you are, knowing that every time you Connect, Listen, Trust, and Act you *are* altering the world by shifting the vibration in which you resonate.

You are powerfully connected to your "inner knowing" as what is real. This shift in awareness and consciousness shifts the context of your life. You are aligning how to resonate to embrace what is real from your *Self*. You find yourself Connecting to the Self of others, you find yourself honoring others, you find yourself speaking from your true *Self*, you find yourself knowing what actions are not aligned with the honoring of You, and you begin to live in a new awareness. You begin to experience life as a place to bring your *Self* to versus allowing all that is here to pull you into its energy. You unfold a journey that continues to align you with your purpose naturally and effortlessly. You transcend the need to fix yourself and those around you to fit the *Mind's* reality. You become someone that is contributing to a higher vibration on the planet. Why you are here becomes the context of your life, as you unfold each day doing what is needed in the duality, knowing that you are your *Self* and the duality is the access to being You. Your daily actions are aligned with your purpose in each moment of "now" that you Trust and Act from your *Self*.

It is knowing that you are only interested in Trusting your *Self* for what there is to know that will have this be a new reality. This new paradigm exists only by virtue of You choosing it to be in existence. There is no existence to this reality without your choice every time you Connect. It is the only access to the new reality.

You are either in the new paradigm or living within the journey of the *Mind*. There are only two tracks giving you your life—the *Mind* or the *Self*. Trust is the access to the new reality; it is you surrendering to your true *Self* as You.

## Maria, Natural Health Coach, Yoga Teacher

Fixing up my house was a huge journey for me. I had quit working and had no money coming in, and I had gotten from *Self* to fix up my house. Now this really didn't make sense to me, I mean let me put it this way, Suze Orman wouldn't have done it. I had a lot of *Mind* chatter about it, and I would talk to Indira about it and she would just say, "This is your journey now." So I would take the Actions I got to take when I Connected to my *Self*. There were blocks to the process that I didn't even want to work with, like times when the contractor wasn't doing the right job, or someone wasn't doing something right and my *Mind* would just be screaming, "I don't want to do this. I'm going to go broke! I don't want to spend my time doing this. I've got to get a job!" But I kept Trusting what I got from *Self* and walking that journey until it was finished. I really did do so much on my property, and I created a beautiful guesthouse that I rent out for $1,200 per week, which means that it's now a source of income. Best of all, it is a haven for people. I have people staying there right now, and recently they invited me over for a little party to meet some of their friends and I said to them, "You guys look so good!" And they were like, "Well thanks to you! We're so relaxed here and it's so beautiful here!" Those are the kind of comments I get. I feel like the place affects people's health in a positive way, and they often tell me it's the best sleep they've had in a long time, or it's the most relaxed they've been ever. I mean there's a lot of fruit trees on the property, and my guests are free to roam around the property and pick my fruit, so they get an experience of nature and healthful living, just being on the property. I created an organic haven. There are no chemicals used here, and everything in the guesthouse is organic and healthy. I've been renting it out for two years and the place attracts a lot of honeymooners—it's very romantic. It was a huge accomplishment to create this on my own and then to maintain it because the property is about an acre and a half. It's something I never would have done if I had not Trusted what I got from Connecting to my *Self*.

## The Practice of Trust

In this step you are holding all of what is unfolding or occurring in your life as your journey. You have made a shift from life "doing it to you" to one in which you are the one who set-up the situations and circumstances to transcend the *Mind's* views to Trusting your *Self* for what there is to know about what is occurring. You are activating your *Self*—the "radio station" of your *Self* for what there is to know—because *any* knowing of what is occurring will only come from the *Mind*. The *Mind* is designed to ensure you never know your true *Self* and to protect you from the illusions of perceived fears of lifetimes where you had situations that evoked the "vows" and "karmic energies" you embody vibrationally and energetically.

You are holding this as the reality that you Trust and bringing forth the "knowing" that when you Trust what is there from your *Self* you are transcending the "karmic energies" of the *Mind* to have a new energy be what vibrates as You. In this energy, you will honor your *Self* and those around you. You will evoke the Actions that will unquestionably have you come from your *Self* and honor the *Self* of another. You activate this duality as a real and tangible part of your life. You bring into existence the "knowing" that this is the journey that there is to tend to and all will be well. You activate a dimension of life called energy, and you begin to Trust energy as a real part of your existence as a human being. You begin to know yourself as a spiritual being on a spiritual journey and to honor that You as the real you.

You hold what is unfolding, to presence the distinction between the journey from the *Mind* and the journey from *Self* and to choose *Self* as what you Trust. You are connected to *all* of the *Mind's* views, thoughts, and opinions, and you choose your *Self* as what you will Trust. This step is profound for it is here that you realign your vibration with its highest truth, for you to honor and Act on.

You are continuing to hold the energy vibrating from Connecting and Listening to now Trust what is being communicated in the energy, and in doing so, you can distinguish the *Mind* and the *Self* as two distinct dimensions.

In the step of Trusting, you are developing your muscle in seeing the *Mind's* energy and drive to create your reality. You are seeing it as your *Mind*. This powerful contextual shift allows you to strengthen your Connection to your *Self*—it is in seeing the *Mind* that you can see your *Self* more powerfully and clearly. In Trust you are in the duality. You are being with the duality; you are releasing the *Mind* and allowing your *Self* to be what is real. You are creating a new context that you are not your Mind. You are holding the duality of both and choosing Self. It is a powerful moment of "now."

This is a powerful moment when Trusting your Self disappears the energies of fear, concerns, and worry. There is never worry, concern, or fears from our Self. Anytime you experience any worry, fears, or concerns, you have just activated a "karmic energy" which is in the Mind's journey or reality.

In this moment you hear your Self clearly, your Self occurs as real. You hear what there is to know as what is real. You embrace this as your truth. You Trust simply because you experience it as your Self. This takes a strength in defining your Self. It is only you who can do this. In this journey no one can make you do this. This is an individual journey. This journey is the journey of activating your Self. You cannot have this happen through learning, osmosis, or someone doing it for you. It is only through you choosing your Self as real that this shift in reality occurs. This is a shift that you develop as you choose to know that you are not your Mind, and when you Connect, Listen, Trust, and Act, you are honoring your Self why you came here.

You are now in the awareness of your Self as you. It is powerful, it is real, it exists. You bring your awareness to your Self. You experience your Self. You hear your Self. It is very different. You are in an energy of deep love, deep compassion, and deep joy. You are here with you as your Self, and you are at home. You are at peace, you are in the "knowing" that "all is well," you are in the "knowing" that you can Trust You. It is an existential moment of "now."

## In the Energy of the Eternal You "All Is Well"

In the energy of "all is well" you are at peace. All that exists in the current paradigm vibrates as an illusion of what is real. It is related to for what it is, a place in which to unfold your *Self*. The people in your life, your job, making money, paying bills are all in that moment inside of "all is well" for you are not in the *Mind's* truths. In this place you can allow the energy of "all is well" to be a truth, and in that moment there is a shift in consciousness for what actions there are to be in and what there is for you to know at that moment. This is activated from the energy of "all is well"—it is a shift in how the energy vibrates. When you take those actions, they will be in the energy of "all is well." You are not taking the actions in order to produce a result or to make it in the world that pulls you back into the current paradigm of the *Mind*.

The *Mind* will always operate from the way it reacts to information, situations, events, and people. It is a mechanism designed to have something be at least slightly wrong up to majorly wrong. There is always something to be changed or fixed or survived. This is the complete opposite of the energy of *Self*.

These illusions from the *Mind* keep us within the experience of not being honored. When we have our actions be about our survival and our own needs, we are disconnecting the energy that our *Self* is here for—which is to have actions that come from creating our connectedness and the sharing of the planet as one.

This shift in awareness *must* occur for humanity to move forward. Being someone who is organized only around making money and climbing to the top will no longer vibrate as our truth. Being someone who discriminates will no longer occur as our truth. The energy of *Self* is the energy that is now here to be unfolded. It is why this conversation is arising on the planet.

We are moving into an era when the change we need cannot come from the current paradigm. It is only when each of us has the courage to step outside of how our *Mind* operates that we will bring *Self* forth. In this new reality, what we Trust and Act on will go beyond what we were taught to do, what is viewed as right or wrong, and how others perceive us. When we trust our *Self*, our *Mind* will not be a barrier to our fullest *Self*-expression. When our actions come from our highest *Self*, there is no dishonoring—it is not about us versus them. It is simply when we are Trusting our *Self*, we will bring to the world what we came here to act on.

As you Trust your *Self*, you become comfortable in your own skin. You are comfortable in who you are; you are not pulled into having to fit into the lifestyle that is considered "right" or "better than" or "superior to" anyone else. The energy of this paradigm does not consume you and take up your life like the current paradigm of the *Mind*. It is now time to embrace your true *Self* and make the impact you came to make in the world.

## You Can Unquestionably Trust That You and Others Will Be Honored

The freedom to be this *Self* comes from knowing that you are honoring others as well as your *Self*. There isn't any action you get to take from your *Self* that will dishonor anything; it therefore gives you the place in which to always Connect to "What is there for me to know about being my *Self* in this situation?" The step of Trusting is making the choice to honor knowing that the moment you chose to Trust your *Self* you shifted into a reality of honoring.

Imagine lawyers, Connecting, Listening, Trusting, and Acting. Imagine politicians Acting from their *Self*. Imagine teachers and parents Acting from their *Self*. Imagine spouses Acting from their *Self*. In this paradigm wars cannot exist because it will be impossible to fight another from your *Self*. This is the new reality unfolding.

You will begin to approach any situation from the "knowing" that you *can* operate from your highest *Self*. This "knowing" shifts your overall experience of what life can be for you. You live in a new reality that at any time you can switch from your *Mind* to your *Self* through the act of Connecting—this "knowing" brings forth the answers that are unique to you and with that a peace and ease in how you approach life no matter what life brings to your doorstep.

You are now organized to be your *Self* as a way of life. You begin to know your *Self* through Trusting your *Self*. You know that this is a choice that you can activate at any moment. You begin to have another experience of why you are here—this "knowing" keeps you from drowning in the *Mind's* fears from the unexpected shifts that occur in life.

You will be in life bringing your *Self* to those around you, and they will find themselves operating in a different vibration simply because you are emitting a different energy than the *Mind*. You activate a force of energy that shifts you and others to an experience of their true *Self*. You will be the catalyst for others to vibrate at a different frequency. As you shift your vibration, it disconnects the "karmic energies" and "set-ups" you have with those around you.

You find yourself bringing a deep love and compassion to people, not from trying to do it or from thinking you need to do it, but simply by being in a different energetic vibration. Each action is transcending the *Mind's* energies to bring forth the energy of *Self*.

You find your relationships naturally flowing in a new vibration where the joy of being together is not one that you are "working on" but is rather unfolding as a natural expression of your *Selves*.

## ⤢ 7 ⤣

# Act: Transcending the Mind to Honor Your *Self*

By taking the Actions you got from Connecting, you transcend the *Mind's* absolute control and honor your *Self*. You could say this is "where the rubber meets the road." The *Mind* will have a lot to say about what you got in your Connections. It will also argue for doing something else, not doing it fully, or create circumstances around you to not do it at all.

The step of Acting is the ongoing struggle to confront the *Mind* and choose *Self*. When you Connect, Listen, Trust, and then encounter Act, you will be confronting the *Mind's* attempt to reclaim control. The step of Acting is an affirmation that in this moment of "now" you have transcended the *Mind's* control to honor your *Self*.

This allows you to walk the journey You are here for. You came for experiencing your own magnificence as you walk your journey on earth.

In Acting, you are saying, "I am not my *Mind*, I am a source of divine truth." The step of Acting is the journey of you claiming your *Self*. To Act is to say "I am integrating my *Self* into the physical realm for what I am here to be and presence in my life —to take the Actions I get from Connecting." Accepting Listening and Trusting marks the final clarity in knowing who you are. It is no longer a struggle with the *Mind*, it is you Acting from your *Self*.

By Acting on what you get from your *Self*, you are intentionally and decidedly choosing the *Self* as You. This is free choice. This is what it means when we say we have free choice—it is the freedom to choose our higher *Self* as who we are. This choice is not coming from a "have to," "should," "it is good or right to," or any of the other things we tell ourselves when we feel like we must do certain things to fit in or make it in life. It is a choice to live your life honoring the Actions you have gotten from your *Self*, not the actions emanating from the *Mind*. This path is a different blueprint for your life, separate and distinct from the path and blueprint from your *Mind*.

When you take the Actions from your *Self*, you are aligning yourself with your authentic journey. When you align yourself with your authentic journey, life is in a different vibration and energetic flow. When you have aligned yourself with your authentic journey, life becomes a natural unfolding with your purpose. You experience the duality as a natural way of life. You are holding the *Mind* as a dimension of you while "seeking into" the "happenings" in your life for what is there to see about you and the journey you chose to experience this lifetime from your *Self*.

You hold in your energetic realm the knowing of your *Self* as real and have this as a place to Connect to on a dime. You go through your journey with another sense available to you. Some people refer to this as your "sixth sense," or your intuitive "inner knowing." It is the guide for everything that is unfolding. When you Trust the

Connection you are guided to take, the Actions will displace the fear, concern, and worry so that your journey opens you up to the fullest experience of your *Self*. You find yourself taking Actions outside of the *Mind's* realm of who it knows you to be.

You are on a journey to release the "karmic energies" that keep you separate, keep your heart closed, and keep you disconnected from divine love as a natural self-expression. The *Mind* has zero interest in you taking Actions from your *Self*. The *Mind* is only interested in controlling your life to repeat the "karmic energies" you have in place. The actions the *Mind* wants you to take will assure these energies will keep repeating. It will have you do what it deems relevant and important in life. You defy the logic of the *Mind* when you Act on what you have claimed as YOU. It is a glorious moment!

### Ann, Business Owner

I had owned a company for twenty years, when I decided to bring in a partner, which made me only a part owner in the company. I had been very challenged in going from being a full owner to being a part owner, and that made our relationship very rocky from the beginning, and especially about a year and a half into it. What I was Connecting to was how to be in partnership with this man who had bought into my company. So I was asking, "What do I need to know about my journey with my partner?" The revelatory moment was learning to distinguish when my *Mind* was at work being in control. That's a big one for me; my *Mind* energy is all about controlling and having

*(continued)*

everything be my way. This actually served me very well for most of my life. But it wasn't serving me now with my partner. So what happened was that my partner was having a conversation with someone, and I was about to jump into that conversation, but instead I just stopped and got present to the fact that my *Mind* was about to do what it always does. So instead of doing anything, I just stopped. What became instantly clear to me was that what needed to happen would just show up by itself, without me needing to do or say anything. So I put that into practice and Acted on it. The experience that I started to have was one of seeing what's next, waiting to see what there is to do next instead of just jumping into the fray. It provided a lot of freedom for both my partner and me. But as I continued to Connect to my *Self*, what happened is almost unbelievable to me. It's very interesting because the other thing that became clear about my business once I started Connecting about partnership was that it was not actually a partnership. I got very clearly, that in reality, I no longer owned my business. This other man owned the company, and I didn't anymore. There's a very interesting dynamic that happened when I really got that down deep in my gut. What's interesting about it was that I was actually fine with that. There was a certain huge relief about it. Best of all, it allowed for other things to show up. Because what I had been doing was trying to maintain control over something I no longer had control over—and that took a lot of energy and time and effort and focus to do. Interestingly enough in that moment, what that allowed for was for me to get into action around other things, like making more sales. I was trying to control everything instead of letting my partner do what he should have been doing, which was managing operations. What's happened is that my having stopped trying to control everything made for a much better partnership. I was much more available for my partner to come to me with questions, and the things he needed, and he listened to me more now that I was no longer trying to control everything. In the course of doing that, in just a few days I booked about $1.2 million in business! That was unheard of for me. When I really looked at it, it was not just a control piece, or operations; what happened was that I've stopped letting my *Mind's* energy run the show, I allowed the vibration of my *Self* to inform my decisions, and I took Action on those things I was getting from my *Self.*

## Developing Your Power to Act

Your power to Act is enhanced as you develop your ability to know your Mind and your Self as two separate and distinct energies. You begin to tell the difference in the tone, resonance, and vibration of the two. You begin to have the Mind and its energy be simply a dimension of you. You will have access to not being pulled into the Mind's drive to bring the logic of what it wants. You begin to quiet the Mind and have it be in the background. You begin to hear your Self more loudly, and you begin to "seek into" the energy of your Self for more and more of what there is for you to know. As you develop this muscle, your Self becomes an open channel for communication, a new and reliable dimension, that is clear, precise, and has an energy and speaking that is unique to your Self and not the Mind. You shift the vibrational space around you, and people begin to know that you are distinct. You evoke the energy of being connected to your Self.

When the Actions you are taking are coming from your *Self*, you live in a new reality where your awareness of who you are is shaped by your *Self*. You bring to your life an awareness of a force of energy that is first Connected to who you are and why you are here. This energy is one that pulls you into being your *Self*. When you are bringing your *Self* to life first, life occurs weirdly when you are not. You begin to feel different if you are annoyed, upset, or going to the *Mind* to deal with people—it begins to feel uncomfortable. This shift in awareness can be a guide to being your *Self* and not your *Mind*. You are so tuned into your *Self* as you, and when you are not being this you, you know it is your *Mind*. You then disconnect the *Mind*, release the energies, and Connect for what there is to know about the energies that are disconnecting you from your *Self*.

This is a contextual shift between you and the world. It is no longer only the you of your *Mind* in your life. When the you of your *Self* in *not* who you are Acting from, creating the energy of honor, you have the experience of feeling lost, alone, and disconnected from life.

In this state change, this paradigm shift, you become someone who is living in the "knowing" that each moment is a new moment to Act on from your *Self*. In this state change, life is now designed around having each moment be a moment to experience your *Self*. When your thoughts are not aligned with experiencing your *Self*, but rather an opinion or conversation about another person from your *Mind*, a "karmic energy" has kicked in for you. This is an immediate flag to check in and Connect, Listen, Trust, and Act from your *Self*. It is a trigger that you can Act from your *Self* rather than your *Mind*. Each moment becomes a manifestation of your *Self* as an expression of who you are and why you are here. You become someone who wants to Act from your *Self* and seeks to Act from your *Self*. You now organize your life to do what is needed to Act from your *Self*. This is the natural and effortless nature of how you become about you and life and the people around you.

## You Live in a New Awareness That Acting from Your *Self* Is YOU

This way of living life is propelled by an awareness that acting from your *Self* is You. You begin to experience life as a vehicle for *You*. You are shifting and releasing "karmic energies" as a way of living. You are Trusting and Acting on the communication from your *Self* and this shapes You; even if the *Mind's* relationship to you is the opposite, which *is* usually the case.

I'll use myself as an example. I have lived in an energy of not being loved, when in reality so many people love me—this "karmic energy" is deep and powerful for me. It makes me want to stay away from people, but my *Self* is always pulling me into being with people. This is a duality I am holding each day in each moment of "now." In my experience of living in a new truth, I am always in each moment of "now," evoking what there is for me to know about Acting from what I am getting to do. I keep myself seeing and experiencing how the *Mind* has created fear, hopelessness, and heightened feelings of "it's not worth it when I act from my *Self*." Building this awareness *is* my journey. It is not a destination. This is the journey I am here to live, and this awareness is also the journey we are all here to live.

When we die, our *Body* is here and our *Mind* and our *Self* are separated. It is the *Self* that becomes once again a force of energy and vibration void of the *Body* and the *Mind*. It experiences all that it has experienced in the last journey. This is why the duality of the *Mind* and *Self is* what we came here for: as you engage in this journey, you are in the journey of your life. Your Actions come from this journey.

## You Shift the Energy in How You Vibrate to Align with the "Universal Consciousness"

When you take the Actions you get to take from your *Self* through Connecting, you are shifting your energy in how you vibrate to align with the "Universal Consciousness." We are all energy; we vibrate in a tone and resonance of our highest *Self*. When we honor that *Self* by taking the Actions that are there to Act on from our *Self*, distinct from our *Mind*, we have aligned with the "Universal Vibration" of a divine and powerful force of love and honor. We are emulating the eternal nature of our *Self*, and we are now in alignment with the "Universal Consciousness" where all that wants to unfold naturally and effortlessly can and will arise.

Knowing this as a truth allows you to simply live your life within the journey of your *Self* distinct from your *Mind*, knowing that being organized to Act from your *Self* will have the situations occur for you to be who there is to be in each moment of "now." You don't have to worry or figure out your life, or strive to be what the *Mind* thinks you need to and should be. It does not take away from what inspires you or what you are currently doing—it simply allows the part of you that is vibrating as your highest *Self* to align with the universe. You are now in a vortex of energy where life will bring what is wanted and needed to experience your *Self*. You are one, in an energetic flow, with how the universe aligns. You are emitting a frequency that affirms your divine nature, and as this frequency resonates in a unique tone and vibration, it is in a harmonic relationship with the universe . . . You become one with the universe.

## Integrating Your *Self* into the Physical Dimension

Every time you take Actions from your *Self*, you have transcended the *Mind's* truth that the physical realm is what is real. The intellectual knowledge of this does not produce a shift, it only becomes something the *Mind* knows as true, but it has no impact on your experience of your life as different. It is *only* when you Connect, Listen, Trust, and *take* the Actions you get to Act on that you then transcend the current reality to have a new reality. Without the Actions there is no integration of your *Self* into the physical dimension.

Without taking the Actions there will be a deep Connection to your *Self*, but the shift in how you vibrate and resonate in alignment with your highest *Self* is *only* experienced when your day-to-day living is organized around taking daily Actions from your *Self*.

When you Act from your *Self* as naturally as you Act from your *Mind*, you get to be in a vibrational force of energy where who you are is now in a *Body* using the *Mind* to be in service of your journey. You experience yourself differently. You hold the *Mind* as a separate part of you. You experience the You of your highest *Self* and are in the experience of being in the joy and honor of this *Self*. It is a real experience. You know and relate to your *Self* as an energy where you experience honoring life around You.

You seek the Actions to keep you in the journey of your true *Self*. You are tuning into the "radio station" of your *Self*. All of what needs to be unfolded from the new paradigm emerges to Act on. Your relationships begin to shift from being from the *Mind* to being from *Self*. You and those you are in relationship with shift, as you are now in alignment with your journey being given from your *Self*.

You find yourself living a life that is unfolding from the Actions taken from your *Self*. You experience this as you honor this journey and bring this out as what you choose to live. You discover that you are more organized around the things that bring you the most joy. You find yourself disengaged from the dimension of the physical realm that keeps you on the hamster wheel, going around and around, having no experience of the true joy of life. You experience yourself trusting life, and the universe, and allowing what is happening to be the unfolding of the journey. You experience life around you as a function of your journey, not what is right or wrong with the world.

You are at peace with what happens and what does not happen. You release all need for expectations and for results driven by the *Mind*. Your life unfolds from simply the Actions you get to take from Connecting.

## You Shift the Context of Your Life from Being a Human Being to Being a Spiritual Being

As your Actions in life unfold from your *Self*, you begin to experience yourself as a spiritual being on a spiritual journey. You experience the dimension of yourself as a human being, not as the context of your life, but as the gift and opportunity for you to bring forth your true and highest *Self*. Your thoughts shift from the thinking of the *Mind* to the "knowing" of your *Self*. You experience yourself naturally seeing life through the lens of your highest *Self*. You are here on the planet for the gift of the opportunity your *Self* is here to impact in each moment of now. You resonate in the knowing of your highest *Self*, and you bring forth that *Self* in life with the people around you. Life is designed around the joys of the moment, distinct from the drive to get to the illusion of the *Mind's* creation.

It is a new paradigm. You are bringing your *Self* to the planet to experience making an impact in simply being your *Self*.

As this becomes a way of living life, you release all of the *Mind's* vibration and truth of who you are. You release the "karmic energies" that are housed in the *Mind*. You are organized around seeking into your *Self*, and in doing so, you keep transcending the illusions and fear of the *Mind's* truths about who you are, what is real, what is possible, what is needed in order to be okay, and what defines you in relationship to life and others, to the "inner knowing" of your *Self*. The *Mind* is now in service to You. There is no place for the *Mind* to operate as real; instead it is powerfully related to the journey of *Self* as what is real.

This is a state change for the current reality to have very little or no impact on what you are Acting on and what you are choosing as the journey of your life. This is monumental. The choice to Act from *Self* leads you to live outside of the need to fit in or belong, spend more than you can afford or need, or take on jobs that the *Mind* thinks you should do—but rather within taking those actions that are from what your *Self* is here to do. It is a total shift from having actions that define the *Mind's* relationship to what should be happening. When we are all in this journey, we will be being and doing who we came to be for the planet.

In this new energy you create a vortex where the flow of life unfolds naturally. You are now given by your *Self*. You find yourself unable or unwilling to act outside of your *Self*. The *Mind* has little or no say in what is unfolding. You are within the energy where the act of releasing the *Mind* is one which is dealt with as a way of life. You are in life releasing the *Mind* to Act from your *Self* as a state change in what your life is about.

## To Act: Knowing That Your *Self* Is Presencing What There Is to Act on in Each Moment

In the step of Acting you bring forth a "knowing" that your *Self* is presencing what there is to know to Act on in each moment of "now." You have Trusted that your *Self* is who you are, and you have activated the "knowing" that your *Self* is here to presence what there is to Act on in each moment to be your true *Self*. This is a state of being. It exists as a state of knowing your *Self* as your *only* reality. It exists as a new realm you have surrendered yourself to. You have brought forth a new state of being as a human being. You have identified and Trusted your *Self* as where you have your actions come from. Your Trusting of your *Self* is not a matter of the *Mind* but of You.

You have developed a keen Listening for your *Self*. You are at home with your *Self's* vibration and resonance. You have surrendered to your *Self* and have trusted your *Self* as a state you have brought forth by your own choice to know yourself as not your *Mind*.

You are becoming at home with your *Self* distinct from your *Mind*. Your Listening for your *Self* is what you are claiming and tending to. Your sense of "knowing" your Self distinct from your Mind is yours. You are unwilling to have the Mind be You because you are and have trusted your Self as You. The Mind's energy is in the background, as your Self becomes a stronger presence in your Listening.

In creating and Trusting the "knowing" of your Self as you, you have embodied a new truth, as energy, that when your Actions come from your Self all will always be well. Your Self will always unfold a life that honors you. In this is a sacred energy in which you have given yourself over to your Self and become someone who is Listening for what there is from your Self to Act on. You begin to develop and empower your Self for its "knowing" as what you are willing to live your life from. You create for yourself a life lived from your Self, you know that having your Actions come from your Self will be your best life. From the Mind these Actions could appear to be illogical or concerning. It is this depth of Trust, and knowing that your are *not* your Mind, that you confront as you take the Actions you get to take from Connecting.

You are embracing the duality. You are dealing with the Mind's "karmic energies," struggling to release them as you Connect, Listen, Trust, and Act from your Self. It is a powerful place to be in. You are confronting all the fears of the Mind to Act from your Self. It is your own journey to honor your Self and not the Mind. It is what creates the shift in vibration at a cellular level. You are shifting the cellular structure in how you vibrate and resonate. Your life is now organized around the duality. It is the new state of being that you are now housed in as your life. The duality becomes the access to the journey you chose to experience.

You begin to organize your day from the Actions you get to take from Connecting to your *Self*. You are in a world where your life is an integration of your *Self*'s energy and vibration. Your relationships, your job, your finances, your family, your partner, your body are all aligned with the journey of your *Self* as you have your days get organized around those Actions that come from Connecting, Listening, Trusting, and Acting for your *Self*

As you begin this journey and have your life given by this new reality, you experience more and more of your life coming from your *Self* as you Act from your *Self* not your *Mind*. You find yourself effortlessly not wanting to have the foods that do not honor your *Body*. You bring forth love in the face of anger when confronted in relationships. Your Trusting of life to be there for all that you need is heightened. You transcend the deep fear of not having money to knowing that you will be taken care of, as you bring an integrity to having your Actions come from your *Self* daily.

You are organized for a life that is from your *Self* as your life; your new reality is why you are here—it is now the life you are choosing to live.

## How Acting Alters Your Life

In this step you experience the peace of knowing you have now altered your life and your reality to that of your true *Self*, your best *Self*. You are no longer of the world, but you are in the world as You. You experience a "knowing" of your *Self* as "all is as it needs to be." You embrace how you look; what you have; what you do; and how your life is, with no loss of self-respect or self-esteem. You are in the moment understanding that your life is now organized around the knowing of your *Self*, and your Actions are coming from your *Self* not your *Mind*. You are at peace as you continue to struggle with the duality.

You wake up each day disengaging the *Mind*'s pulling of you into the reality determined by the *Mind*'s view of you, the world, life, and what is happening. You declare "happenings" and "set-ups" as you seek into what life has brought to you to transcend from the *Mind*. You are bringing the journey of your *Self* forth as life keeps bringing you the situations and circumstances to transcend the *Mind* and Act from your *Self*. You deal with life from the duality of the *Mind* and the *Self*. You can release the *Mind*'s pull for you to fit in, to be one of the many, to have how the *Mind* sees life and how you should be become your reality. You can disengage this energy as you have your days and life be organized around Connecting, Listening, Trusting, and Acting.

You are at home with not relating to the *Mind* as you. You Trust that you are more than what the *Mind* says you are, and this allows you to release the *Mind*'s survival and control.

You become willing to keep Trusting your *Self* in the face of the strength of the *Mind* and its fear. You experience the fear—you hold the fear and the unknown as a dimension of you—but you keep confronting the truth that it is not You as you Connect and take the Actions you get to take. It is only when you keep Acting from your *Self* in the face of the deep "karmic energies" of the *Mind* that you keep transcending the *Mind*-driven experience of life.

To live from your highest *Self* is only possible through a new reality, a new paradigm of not relating to how the *Mind* is designed to keep you in the experiences of fears, which from the *Mind*, are real. The reality of the *Mind* leads us to end our marriages, stay in marriages where we are abused, attack and kill each other, abuse children, discard family members, and hold on to experiences of being hurt. We live in realities that keep us separate and removed from the people we love—it is truly unbelievable how much the *Mind* drives our reality. We are so accustomed to living this way that we have no idea there is another reality available to us. This reality can only exist through a new reality. It cannot be accessed through the *Mind*.

## You Begin to Have an Honoring of Your *Self*, You Live in the Love of Who You Are, as You Are

To be within the love of who you are, as you are, is the access to everything. You loving you, as you are, as an eternal energy, allows you to embrace how you look, what you weigh, where you are, what you are doing, without dishonoring your *Self*. You are and have activated your *Self* as the energy of total honor void of your physical form. You bring forth the energy of living in a vibration where what you are doing is not defining who you are, for when you are in the energy of your *Self* as you, you release the *Mind's* connection to you in the physical world as real. You become someone whose actions from your *Self* unfold the journey you came here to Act on as what you honor. You recontextualize what you are here to do. You are not using up your time trying to do the things that the *Mind* wants you to do: to relate and belong and fit into the physical realm. You may be taking those actions, but it comes from the energy of your *Self*.

Tending to the *Body* becomes the first energy that arises when you live from the new reality. The vibration of the *Body* arises as Actions to tend to from your *Self* such that the actions around your *Body* become aligned with what serves your *Body*.

What naturally comes up for you to do around your *Body* becomes an energy that evokes the Actions that bring an integrity to your *Body*. From the new paradigm the *Body* is the vessel for the journey. From the new reality the *Body* is the strongest energy to honor and Act on.

You are altering the realm where the honoring of your *Body* is not just actions to take as you tend to the *Body*, but rather you begin to vibrate in an energy where the *Mind's* truth about your *Body* is now aligned with honoring how your *Body* is. The way you look becomes the expression of your *Self*. You find a love for your *Body* that comes from the cells' vibration, from within, from a "knowing" that how you look is the joy of being You. This energetic shift in vibration and resonance is an access to a new realm from which to be You in the world.

As these energies become a reality, you live and experience your life as a journey from how your true *Self* vibrates. You begin to want to Act from your *Self* in as many situations in your life as possible. You become someone who sees the difference in living from your true *Self*. You become someone who knows when you are in your *Self*, and when you are in your *Mind* in an instant. The you of your *Mind* begins to disappear as you transcend the "karmic energies" the *Mind* is running on. You experience the vibration of your true *Self* as you begin to know that as You. You are in life for the journey of your *Self* as it becomes the only reality you experience.

## Linda, Sales Representative

I am a dancer, but I usually just dance when I'm in a play, like musicals and things like that. I find dancing is a great way of expressing and generating joy for myself. So when I started Connecting, I got a very specific message that said I don't have to just dance when I'm in a musical, I can do it for myself. I don't even have to have an audience. There's no reason why I can't choreograph my own dances, and practice them, and enjoy them, so I Trusted and Acted on what I got to start doing. At the gym I go to, there's a dance studio, and now every morning I go there, and I practice dancing, and I love it. And afterward the whole day just feels great because I have done something for my *Self* and generated this joy—these feelings that are always inside but I just never let them out. To take it one step further—I recently auditioned for a play—I didn't get the part I was auditioning for, but the director asked me to choreograph the dancing in the show, which I've never done before. But I got from my *Self* that this is the next step for me. This is opening up a whole new world for me where if I hadn't trusted my *Self,* and realized that I could dance on my own and develop my own choreography, I would never have been confident enough to accept this role of teaching other people and having them perform it. This was something I got from my *Self* and I Acted on it, and it's brought me so much joy.

## You Activate the "Inner Knowing" That You Are Eternal

In Acting on what you have gotten from *Self*, you have activated the "inner knowing" that you are eternal. This energy is the core essence of the new paradigm. The "knowing" of your eternalness shifts the experience of life and the people in your life into a new context. This "knowing" allows the *Mind* to take a backseat. It allows the *Mind* to be as it is designed—a tool, a mechanism that is there to be of service to your *Self*. The activation of the "inner knowing" that you are eternal is the driver of the new paradigm. You shift the vibrational nature of your existence to a new truth. This truth transcends the current paradigm and creates a new paradigm that your eternal nature is what is real and who you are. The activation of the "inner knowing" that you are eternal allows you to hold the You of your highest *Self*. This knowing allows you to hold the world and life around you as a dimension where you seek into what is unfolding as your journey.

Taking Actions that defy our fears and concerns will allow for a shift in humanity that is propelled by each of us acting from our *Self*. This is the new reality of life.

When you can Act in the face of the fears of the *Mind*, you can honor your *Self* and its journey. You become the change in your life that your *Self* wants to have happen. You can move through horrific situations, and not have the *Mind* keep you in situations that dishonor you. You can rise to your highest *Self* and claim the journey you know within you is who you are. You can bring your unique You to the planet for what you came here to contribute and fulfill as You.

There is a contextual shift in life when the *Mind* disengages the truth that fear is real and your *Self* allows you to move into your life and Trust and Act on those things that you got in a Connection that forward your experience of your *Self* and your journey. The vibration and energy you emit when you Act in the face of the *Mind's* fears not only transcends and shifts life around you, but also the world. As energy, you do alter the global vibration and beyond. You live in the experience of a life that transcends the physical realm as your Actions from *Self* arise, as the *Mind's* truth of what is real alters. It is a new journey that redefines our very existence.

## You Develop a Trust in Your *Self* That Shapes a Unique Journey

The Trust you develop in your *Self* becomes larger than the life your *Mind* knows to be true. All is available in the Trusting of your *Self*. The Trust is so vast and so great that the world becomes the playground for any and all Actions from your *Self*. It is a remarkable journey. It is now in the Trusting of your *Self* that this unique and powerful experience arises. How you are with your family, how you are with your children, how you are with your spouse or partner, how you are about who you are, all shifts vibrationally. As you develop a Trust in your *Self*, you begin to Act on things that the *Mind* does not have as its reality. You begin to Trust the intuitive You—its vastness and its dimension—for being in the oneness of life, for its energy that is here to impact humanity. You handle the basics of life as an ongoing unfolding as you shift from the *Mind's* reality to Acting on what you get to do from your *Self*. Life is experienced as nonlinear. No longer are you in a linear journey where there is a step-by-step progression; instead you exist in a nonlinear vibration, where all of what you are doing is moving you into being more of your Self, as you Trust and Act from your Self. You are not waiting to get somewhere, you are not waiting to be something—you are bringing to your life your highest Self in each moment of "now." From the people around you, your job, or what you are doing to the conversations you are in—the Universe aligns with the journey as you find yourself taking Actions that have unexpected situations arise in life. It is a unique journey that is coming from a new paradigm of how life is lived.

You develop a deep compassion for the duality. You know the duality is the journey. You become related to the duality as life. You seek into the duality as the access to your journey. You discover dimensions of the duality as you hold the energy of the Mind as separate and distinct from you. You allow yourself to have a compassion for the duality, for it is only with compassion that you can confront the Mind's truth and know it as it is and not as You. This journey requires a profound relationship to your Mind as separate from your Self. It allows you to embrace the Mind's role and purpose and to keep creating the duality as real. It is this claiming and owning of the duality that allows the journey of Self to arise.

As you now live in this realm, you can hold situations from the "inner knowing" that you will Act from your Self. This is a profound shift in consciousness and awareness. You have altered the Mind to be of total service to your Self. In any situation, at any time, you can flip the switch to your Self's "inner knowing" and have that be what you choose to Act on.

The knowing that you will Act from your Self allows you to be in peace, to hold all of what is occurring in life in the "knowing" that you will unfold as your best in any situation when you Act from your Self.

## ≈ 8 ≈

# Death: The Journey of
# *Self* Continues

From the *Mind's* view Death vibrates as the end. It is the end of what the *Mind* knows is real. It is important to note the power of this energy. It keeps your relationship to Death in the energy and vibration of fear, loss, and of all of the experiences that you have when your *Mind* defines your truth.

In the energy of "this is the end," people who have lost loved ones could spend years in the energy of sadness, deep despair, and the hurt and pain of what is experienced as "the end." It is as powerful as the energy of conception and birth, except it has a different vibration in how you experience it, because it leaves you with the illusion of the loss of all of what is real, from the *Mind's* paradigm. This illusion leaves you unable to experience the depth of the extraordinary life you have lived. No matter what you did, you did have an extraordinary life because you lived your journey in the duality of *Mind* and *Self*, whether recognized or not. This is not the experience from the *Mind*. The *Mind* accounts for what you did, and what you didn't do, or accomplish, or fulfill, and in doing so leaves you once again in the energy of what dishonors you rather than what honors you. You are pulled into all of the emotions of the *Mind*—the void and the disconnect from the human experience. It is truly the end.

It has to be set up this way because when you die with these experiences as real, it keeps in place the "karmic energies" of your disconnect from your *Self* and others. It creates the experience of being separate, of being fearful, and of being alone. It is these vibrations that the *Mind* is organized around. From your *Mind* you leave this journey with these truths in place to deepen these energies for the next time around. It reinforces the dimension of the *Mind* that life is about your survival, that you are always alone, and that your innate nature is to defend and protect yourself.

From the *Mind*, you leave this journey once again poised and set up for the next time you are here—you leave with the deep experience that there is an end, that you are alone, and that your experience here, while you did all that you did, still did not fulfill your true *Self*.

In the act of dying from the dimension of your *Mind* as who you are, you strengthen the truth that the *Mind* presences as your reality. You seal more powerfully the reality of the physical world as what is real. You relate to the physical world as the dimension of you that defines who you are and why you are here. Everything the *Mind* says is the truth about your life and journey becomes what you leave resonating as your truth. In this the *Mind* is the driver of your life and journey. It is what you relate to as your measure of your experience of joy, happiness, or fulfillment.

Your experience is still through what the *Mind* has claimed as your life. This leaves you with only the knowing of yourself from your *Mind* rather than the *Self* that chose to experience the journey called your life.

As you leave your life from the energy of the *Mind*, you reaffirm the truth that life is a destination. From the *Mind* you look at your life from the energy of:

What is the life you lived?

What are the things you did and did not do?

What are the things you missed doing that you should have done?

What could you have done if you did it differently?

What could have happened if you did do what you wanted to do, etc.?

All of these thoughts generated from your *Mind* keep in place the pictures of what the *Mind* thinks and feels life is about. It is all what the *Mind* is driving and creating. It holds on to the emotions and feelings that are evoked as you leave thinking it is the "end." This seals the knowing of the *Mind*—that there is a destination and you either fulfilled what the *Mind* thinks and feels it should look like at the destination or you did not. There will always be what did not occur, for the *Mind* is always presencing the truths about what the journey of your life should be like. These powerful impressions are imprinted in your DNA and are always defining the truth about what your life should be like. At Death this is the most powerful resonance, for it is the end and there is no more time to fulfill these impressions evoked by the *Mind*. The desti-nation, like the end, is a moment of "now" that reaffirms your futile effort to be your true *Self*.

In doing all of the above, the *Mind* has ensured its paradigm is what is real. In the duality, the *Mind's* presence and energy are strong here, for, in the physical realm, it is the end of your physical journey. In this dimension the *Mind's* paradigm is reinforced. All of what you needed to do, should do, must have fulfilled, or should have made time to do is validated. Even if you presence that you should have taken more time with the ones you love, it is still in the energy of the *Mind* that there is no more time and something was missing from your life. It was not done the way it should have been done. All this reinforces what the *Mind* is designed to drive in your life: it defines who you are and what you are here for.

## Death through the Journey of Your *Self*

When you Connect to your *Self* and develop a deep "knowing" that who you are is not your *Mind*, but your *Self*, you have a very different relationship to death. Death from the energy of your *Self* is an equally powerful energy that activates a very distinct vibration. You are in the awareness of the eternalness of your journey. It is ever more powerful in this moment of your journey. As you know you are leaving your physical form, you become more Connected to the vibration of your true *Self*, and you are housed and cloaked in the deep "knowing" of the love and honor of your journey. You are in awe of the duality and can experience the fear of the *Mind*, while presencing the love, peace, and joy of the eternal nature of your *Self*. You are in the "knowing" of the gift of life, and in so doing you are simultaneously presencing the honor of the gift of life. You are in the presence of the joy of the journey and the fulfillment of all that you have unfolded. You can presence where you honored your *Self* and have a depth of compassion for the duality that you chose. It is a marvelous time.

In the time of your Death you experience the duality as real and tangible. Just as the *Mind* is a powerful force, so is the energy of your *Self*. In the choice to know your *Self* as who you are, you transcend the *Mind's* truth, bringing forth the vibration and frequency of your *Self* as who you are. This is the moment that most defines your journey—to know your *Self* as who you are, not your *Mind*. The duality becomes the access to your energetic realm, shifting to the frequency and resonance of your divine nature as your true *Self*. You are present to the deep compassion and love for your *Self*.

In the duality you "see" your *Self* as real. You bring forth the awareness of your eternal nature. You are in the realm of energy as real. It becomes the paradigm you know as your truth. You hold the "knowing" that the choice to be your *Self* is why you came and what your life has been about. All of the physical dimension of life becomes the gift where you got to play out your journey. You bring forth the honoring of your journey and all that you have unfolded. You have compassion for where you lived from your *Mind* . The duality gives you access to your true *Self*, your eternal nature, as your only reality.

## This Creates the Dimension of Energy as Real

It is truly in the experience of Death that energy resonates very powerfully as real. It is where the new paradigm vibrates as a truth where the *Mind* is no longer what is real—in the realm of energy. In your Death it is the energy of your *Self* that exists as real. It is your breath, as energy, that leaves your physical form. As you Connect to this "knowing," you can access the force of energy that resonates as your *Self*. You have access to leaving in the "knowing" of the energy of your *Self* as who you are. You can honor your Body for what it has provided you— an experience of your *Self* as energy. The vibration and frequency in which you resonate live in the "knowing" of your *Self* as the journey. You are leaving the physical realm, and in doing so you can embrace the dimension of energy and have this dimension as a source of deep peace and divine presence. You can activate the divine nature of who you are, and in that "knowing" you leave the physical realm as it was designed to be—a pure gift in which you got to discover your true *Self*.

It is in this moment when the duality is the clearest for you—where the *Mind* is in the end and your *Self* is in the eternal nature of your journey—that you can embrace a more powerful connection to your experiences in the physical realm. You can experience the duality in its fullest essence. You can be in the fullness of the journey you chose. You can allow your experiences to resonate for what they were for you: a journey where you got to have the gift of "knowing" your deepest and most divine *Self*. You can hold the world for what it is, an ongoing experience where you get to bring your highest *Self* for what you have brought to the experience of life. You can hold and know your *Self* as deep love and honor for each person and life itself. You can hold your connection to the physical realm as a truly momentous occasion, and you can be at peace in the "knowing" that you did unfold your journey. From your *Self* you will presence where you honored your *Self*. You will leave in the "knowing" of another experience of who you are in the face of the *Mind's* truths of who you are and what you did not fulfill. In this you claim your experiences as your choice. In this choice you are within the awareness of the shift in your energetic realm, as you once again leave the duality in the "knowing" of your *Self* as an energetic force of divine consciousness.

## This Opens Up a View of Life That Transcends the *Mind's* Paradigm

As you embrace Death from the energy of your *Self*, you bring forth an awareness and consciousness that transcend the *Mind's* paradigm. You see the view of it all. You know the truth. You step into your eternal "knowing" of what is real, and in doing so you transcend the *Mind's* paradigm that the physical realm is what is real. You become clear that your eternal journey is who you are. You embrace life as a moment of "now" in your journey. You shift into the new reality and the new paradigm as your only reality. You see the *Mind* for what it is, a tool for your journey. You know that your *Self* is the only paradigm that there is. You are brought to a new view of your *Self*. You embrace this *Self* for its compassion and its love and its honor. You are in awe of who you are; you are in the glory of your true *Self*.

You have the *Mind's* paradigm as the illusion, and you move into the energy of your true journey—the journey of your higher *Self*. In transcending the *Mind's* paradigm, you are experiencing life within the energy and vibration of a deep love and compassion for your *Self*. You find yourself in the experience of deep compassion for where you did and where you did not honor your *Self* or others, knowing that in this awareness you are at peace.

## Death—An Honoring of the Journey the *Self* Came Here to Experience

From the new paradigm of living life from your *Self*, Death is defined as a dimension of the journey you chose to experience. It is a moment in your journey when you get to know the magnificence of your *Self*, as you presence the honoring of the *Self* and the experience you unfolded in the journey of your life.

It is in your Death that you can see the dimensions of your journey and hold all that has unfolded from the totality of your eternal journey. As you seek into your life from the "happenings," "set-ups," and the transcending of the *Mind's* "karmic energies" and patterns, you reveal a journey that includes the physical realm, but is not of the physical realm. It is a remarkable time. You leave your physical form in the "knowing" of who each person you were with was "set up" by you to be in your journey. You can seek into events and situations for what they evoked for you and who you were in them, from the "knowing" that in the duality you were either your *Mind* or your *Self*. You can declare the "happenings" that you unfolded where your *Mind* drove your life and the experiences that you let yourself and others be in as a result of having your *Mind* be the driver of your journey/life. In the moment of your Death all of this is here as a gift to elevate your awareness and shift the vibration and frequency in which you resonate. It is a time of truly being in the gift that you chose at conception—to experience your *Self* in a physical form. It is a time to presence the new paradigm. Time and linearity are not a dimension; in the absence of time you hold a brief moment in which you got to bring forth your *Self* as you embrace the duality of being a spiritual being on a spiritual journey.

## Have All Situations of Death Be the "Set-Up" You Chose to Experience

From the new paradigm of living from your *Self* as your reality, every situation or circumstance in which you die is the "set-up" that you chose to experience. The duality here is very powerful, for from the *Mind* it is inconceivable that a person has "set up" their passing. Why is this so? The *Mind* is organized around the truth that this physical realm is all that exists. Please note that I am not saying that your passing is predestined or planned. Each moment of "now" in the new paradigm is a new moment where the resonance and vibration of what is presenting itself as energy shift and align with a new experience of your journey.

This statement is huge. It takes away any of the *Mind's* vibration that what your *Mind* knows has anything to do with the truth in the new paradigm.

So, what does it mean that all situations of Death are the "set-up" that a person chose to experience? It is so by virtue of it being what has happened. Their passing occurred the way it occurred. Simply that. No more. When you can embrace Death as the "set-up" that person is here to experience, you "honor" their Death.

It is in the honoring of the Death of someone that you allow their passing to be what it is designed to be—a dimension of their eternal journey, an experience that they have now, in their journey, to bring to the ongoing unfolding of their "knowing" of their *Self* more powerfully than their *Mind*.

The moment of Death is a powerful duality. It is a place where the *Mind* is very much related to what is happening from the current paradigm—the paradigm of the *Mind*. It is the end of what is real as the physical dimension, and from the *Mind*, given this is the only paradigm, it evokes deep emotions about what has occurred. Given that life is about the duality, you are always in the experience and knowing that the duality is occurring. You have it be there as a dimension of your life, while simultaneously bringing forth the awareness that your *Self* is in the energy of "all is well."

Due to the *Mind's* vibration, the Death of someone you love is very difficult to hold in the duality, for Death evokes all of your senses: you can no longer see them, you can no longer touch them, you can no longer hear them, you can no longer smell them: their presence is no longer in existence. However, as energy they are more alive and more available to you than ever. This is the new paradigm. From your *Self* you can Connect to what their journey has brought to you and have that vibrate and resonate more than the *Mind's* truth.

Your choice to unfold life from the new paradigm leaves you in the awe and glory of their journey, celebrating all that they have unfolded. It allows you to seek into your "set-up" with them, to declaring their Death a "happening," and to transcend what your journey with them was here to bring forth for both of you. It allows you to have a shift in your energetic realm as you bring this unfolding forth from your *Self*, distinct from your *Mind*. It is about your journey, not the *Mind's* energy, about the reality of how you are to experience Death. It is a powerful moment of "now" for your experience of the duality. From the *Mind*, each situation of Death is designed to evoke an experience for you and for them. When held in this context, it shifts from being something that was done to them and to you. Death, as a "happening," is designed to evoke deep "karmic energies" that are held between those who are still here and those who have left. They are now in another dimension of their relationship to you—one of energy. You are in the physical dimension relating to them from the physical realm. This disconnect creates more sadness and leaves you with the energy of what is evoked in Death as another energy the *Mind* is holding as a truth. When you can seek into their Death from your journey through Connecting and access what it is designed to evoke for you from your *Self*, you release the "karmic energies" and have a more powerful relationship to their journey as it relates to your journey.

### Nigel, Project Manager

I started Connecting for the first time about two weeks after my dad passed away. Connecting helped me to come to terms with losing my dad, and that really impacted me. It wasn't necessarily a specific Connection, but in many Connections I got this experience of peace about it. There had been a lot of pain and grief around my father passing. And then there were a couple of specific Connections where it started to shift that, and I got that my dad will always be with me. There was a real shift from the experience that he is gone, or that he's somewhere that's distant from me, to the experience now that he is always very much with me. In fact, it became less about him not being here physically, and it became—and it's hard to put this into words—but it became less about him not being here and more about that he is actually now more here and more with me than ever before. And that sounds strange, but that is my experience of it.

It is here that it makes sense. It is here that you hold their energy as real. It is here that your journey continues having their energy shaping who you are and why you are here. It is designed to be that way, where they are honored from the eternalness of your journey together, when you will once again connect in the physical realm to continue to unfold what you once held as your journey.

## Transcending the Mind's Truth about Death Is an Access to a Longer Healthier Life

What I am about to say is very different from the current view and occurs only from the new paradigm. Your relationship to Death as a dimension of your eternal journey, and as the continuation of the journey of your *Self*, brings forth a distinct vibration and energy whereby your life can be lived from a place of shifting into the honoring of your *Body*.

This is a very different connection. It is through seeing Death through the lens of the new paradigm that you have a vibrational shift in the frequency in which you resonate in a way that allows you to have access to your *Body* in ways that ensure a longer and healthier life with ease, grace, and effortlessness.

When your cells resonate in a new truth—that Death is a release into a continuation of your journey—you bring forth a new frequency in which your DNA resonates. You shift into the transcending of the *Mind's* truth that there is an end, not from the *Mind's* knowing as in knowledge, but into the energetic shift in your resonance and vibration. The distinction here is that a shift in energy alters the frequency in which you vibrate.

In this "knowing" as your reality, your *Body* becomes aligned with this truth as its reality. Inside of the *Body* being the vessel and vehicle for your journey, you activate the "knowing" of your *Body*—what there is for you to know to allow this journey to unfold in its highest expression. To have this occur will evoke the energies of your *Body* for what is there to honor your *Body*. This vibration will be second nature, inescapable. You cannot evoke this truth, this view that resonates in the new paradigm, and not have your actions around your *Body* be in alignment with this new frequency. If you are living your life from Connecting, Listening, Trusting, and Acting from your *Self*, as a way of life, you will be naturally pulled to honor your *Body*.

As you embrace this paradigm cellularly, you begin to disconnect more of the *Mind's* energy that this is the end. You begin to transcend this energetically, and in doing so, you activate within your cells a resonance and vibration of a new truth that you are unfolding an eternal journey. Your experience of your *Self* becomes more available to you. You begin to embrace life from a "knowing" that lets you hold all of life as a journey from which Trusting and Acting on what you get from your *Self* allows you to release your innate fears and be open to the journey to manifest as it is designed to unfold.

Your Actions from your *Self* become the journey of your life, where there is not an end but a continuation. The presencing of this duality as you continue to transcend your *Mind* begins to redefine who you are and why you are here. You begin to experience your true *Self* and Trust this *Self*. You become someone whose life is a manifestation of the vibration that leaves you and those around you with a deeper "knowing" of who you are. You are within the glory of life and the gift of the journey. This effortlessness is experienced as your vibration is now aligned with and resonating with the "knowing" of your highest truth: You are an eternal being on an eternal journey.

## How the Dimension of Energy Impacts Your *Body* Cellularly

It is important to note that from the new paradigm, the cellular shift in your Body provokes a profound awakening of having your *Body* align itself in a frequency where honoring your *Body* becomes a natural part of your journey. You cannot evoke the "knowing" of your *Self* as an eternal energy without having your *Body* shift into a "knowing" of itself as a dimension of the eternal journey. In this new truth your *Body* begins to activate an energy where what honors and supports the journey of your physical nature is a dominant and necessary part of the journey. In the energy of an eternal being, your *Body* is now organizing itself for the eternalness of this journey. While the *Body* is in the physical journey, there is much to access such that the journey of your spiritual and eternal nature is here for a longer, healthier life with the *Body* truly as the vessel for the depth and length of this experience. It is a symbiotic relationship. Your *Body* comes alive with a vibrancy and a "knowing" of its journey. In this new paradigm, you transcend what is around you that dishonors your *Body* to only embracing what allows it to unfold its journey: to be a vehicle and vessel for the journey of your *Self*.

The awareness of the energy of Death as a dimension of who you are, as an eternal energy, allows you to hold the journey of the eternal vibration. The "knowing" of this as a truth gives you enormous access to a dimension of your *Self* that is not possible to reach through the current paradigm of the *Mind*. In the energy of the *Mind* you are a physical form, and when you die, it is the end.

As energy, you are within the "knowing" that you are vibrating and resonating with the energy of your eternal *Self*. You have access to this as energy and can, at any time, shift the vibration within your *Body* by living this as your truth. In this new paradigm, your access to energy is limitless. You have energy as real. You can relate to your *Self* as energy. You can bring that paradigm forth and have your Actions shape the paradigm that energy can make possible. You can activate the vibration of your true *Self* by simply bringing this awareness forth.

It is important to note that the *Mind* will always be resonating inside of a vibration of controlling and surviving, for this is what the *Mind* does. In Connecting, you will keep bringing forth the awareness of "knowing" that the energy of your *Self is* your new paradigm. This shifts the frequency and vibration in which your *Body* is resonating to emit the truth of your highest *Self*, the highest energy that allows your physical form to be as it was designed to be: a vessel for a remarkable journey of *Self*. Relating to your *Body* from a "knowing" of its journey as a vessel for the *Self* is not done to fix, but simply to honor your *Body*. This understanding reshapes why you have a *Body* and begins to activate the "knowing" of how your *Body* vibrates from the new paradigm.

In this new paradigm, your *Body* is naturally resonating as it was designed to be from its vibration: as a vessel for the journey of your *Self*. In this truth you begin to experience your *Body* not as a thing from the *Mind*, but as an energetic force of vibration and consciousness.

In this new awareness you experience your *Body* as an energetic force of consciousness that can hear and respond through energetic thoughts. When your energy is being evoked from your *Self*, you can *only* be in the honoring of your *Body*. When your thoughts are being evoked from your *Mind*, you are in an antagonistic relationship with your *Body*. From the perspective of the *Mind* the *Body* is only a tool to fulfill what the *Mind* is driving—the survival of life. From your *Mind* there is no honoring, and therefore you find yourself treating your *Body* in ways that dishonor it—not as an intention but *simply* because it is how the *Mind* vibrates.

When you can hold the energy of Death as a dimension of your eternal journey, you can hold your *Body* as it was designed to be from the new paradigm: a magnificent force of energy and vibration that responds when you Trust and Act from your *Self*. From this new paradigm, the *Body is* designed to live and transcend the linear nature of the current paradigm. Aging shifts, healing occurs, and it is all a natural way of life. It truly is a new paradigm.

Living from honoring Death as a continuation of the journey allows for a vibrational shift in how you experience your *Body*. Within your awareness of honoring Death as a continuation of the journey of your *Self*, you begin to experience an "inner knowing" of your *Body* as an energy to honor. You begin to vibrate in the "knowing" of your *Body* and Death as a oneness in your journey. You begin to experience the gift of your physical form as your awareness of your *Body*, and your Death becomes the "knowing" that shapes your eternal journey.

As you begin to honor your *Body*, you begin to honor your Death. You begin to activate the vibration of your life that transcends your physical form and embrace your Death as a dimension of your journey. You experience living from the "knowing" of your *Self* as your paradigm, and you are at peace.

As you live from your *Self* as who you are, you begin to hold your *Body* as it was designed to be: a powerful dimension of your journey. You begin to know that your *Body* is *not* outside of you. You begin to live in a new awareness that you *have* an access to your Death through your *Body*. In this "knowing," Death transcends from the *Mind's* view of fear to a "knowing" of an unfolding of your journey. You begin to know your *Self* as the source of your *Body's* journey—it is one and the same.

Your access to Death is not to fear it, but rather to know that by honoring your *Body*, you can allow your journey here to be one that fulfills the experience of your Death by how you choose to honor your *Body*. This is a profound statement. It is totally outside the current paradigm that is designed to only create fear around Death and a dishonoring of the *Body*.

As you bring forth being at the source of your *Body*, you begin to experience your embracing of Death as a joy, as a moment to celebrate, and as a "knowing" that no matter how you are physically, you have honored the totality of your journey—your *Mind*, your *Body*, and your *Self*.

## A Powerful Energy of Giving You Access to the *Body* as a Vessel for the Journey

Shifting from your *Mind* to your *Self* as your paradigm immediately presences a powerful energy designed to have you unquestionably honor your *Body*. As one embarks on this journey, the *Body* becomes the first energy that arises to honor from *Self*. It must be in this vibration, for without the *Body* you *cannot* unfold your journey.

You begin to confront Connecting, Listening, Trusting, and Acting for that that honors your *Body*. You redefine how your *Body* vibrates. You shift from the *Mind's* view of your *Body* to a divine love for the vibration and resonance of the gift that is called your "*Body*." Your *Body* shifts from being a "thing" to being a source of ongoing honor. You begin to experience this shift in awareness as you Connect, Listen, Trust, and Act on what there is for you to know to honor your *Body* each day. It becomes a remarkable journey. You begin to hold your *Body* as what there is to honor in each moment. This is the experience of a new paradigm.

What and how to act with your *Body* is uniquely shaped by what your *Self* resonates to Act on. This is a paradigm shift, for while there is so much that you can learn about what to do, you naturally find yourself wanting those foods your *Body* needs in a way that is unique to you. You begin a journey of disconnecting what the *Mind* is presencing it wants, to what is being presenced by your *Self* for what there is to eat that honors your *Body*.

Life is not organized around what the *Mind* has learned, or been taught, or simply wants as the things that are best for you. YOU experience the activation of an "inner knowing" of what there is to Act on in each moment of "now" that is needed for You. This is the most powerful and magnificent dimension of this journey. YOU find yourself in love with your *Body* no matter what the world defines as beautiful.

You become at peace with what you look like, the color of your skin, the shape of your *Body*, the natural ease of doing what is needed to honor what your *Body* needs to be in optimum well-being. This becomes the journey that you are organized around. Whatever is occurring that dishonors you, as you transcend all of the *Mind's* energy and embrace the vibration of your *Self*, you are free to release to be You in life. You find yourself naturally embracing the journey of your *Self*, knowing that you are Connecting, Listening, Trusting, and Acting from honoring your *Body* as a way of life.

Having your *Body* aligned with the energy and journey of your true *Self* creates a harmonizing of energy that aligns you with your journey and your purpose. As you activate the vibration and resonance of the frequency that aligns your Body with the journey of your *Self*, you emit energies that allow for a universal alignment with your purpose and journey.

The awareness of your *Mind*, *Body*, and *Self* connection is a tangible vibration that has a reality to its resonance and frequency. Your *Self* is honored as you transcend your *Mind's* relationship to your *Body* and as you activate an honoring of your *Body* as your *Self*.

You become someone who experiences your *Self* as who you are, as the journey of life continues to presence situations and events designed to open up your purpose— who you are and why you are here. At Death you are at peace in the "knowing" of having honored your *Body*, allowing for your purpose to be available to you in each moment of "now" in your journey.

## Purpose—To Have Your Actions in Each Moment of "Now" Come from Your *Self*

I define purpose as having your Actions in each moment of "now" come from your *Self* distinct from your *Mind*.

This is a redefining of the word Purpose. Unlike how Purpose is experienced in the current paradigm, this is not a journey you are predestined to live. Each moment of "now" is a new moment to energetically shift all past and all future from the Mind to allowing what is resonating from your Self be what you Trust and Act on. As a human being living this journey, you will find yourself in the joy of being your Self in each moment. Each moment of "now" in life becomes a new moment to disconnect the Mind's truths about us, life, and what is unfolding to presence a new action that shapes once again who you are and why you are here.

As your life unfolds from this "knowing," what you are here to do, what you are here to be, who you begin to know your Self as unfolds your purpose. In its simplicity, void of the Mind, you are not seeking into the "shoulds," the guilt, the "what-ifs," the lack, or the wrongs—for there are none. You are simply claiming your Self as real and honoring your Self for the journey you are Trusting and Acting on—you begin to embrace life in a new "now." As you embrace Death from the new paradigm, you can hold the duality powerfully as you continue to Trust and Act in each moment of "now," unfolding your Purpose and knowing that you lived your life from your Purpose. You are, therefore, within the honoring of the journey of your life, no matter what experiences you have.

You find yourself organizing your life around what there is to Act on that honors your Body. As this energy becomes a dimension of your life that is real, situations and circumstances arise to Trust and Act on what you need. You are actively taking Actions that you are getting to take from your Self. The physical realm begins to manifest what you need to continue to honor your *Body*. It transcends whether you have money or not, for money is a tool for the journey; it is not what is needed to honor your *Body*. Your *Self* is always resonating in the "now," and as such, you begin to Trust the Actions you get to take. The *Mind's* conversations of what is good or bad to do, or right or wrong, are transcended as your Actions in the physical realm become the new patterns you embody that honor your physical form.

## Death as a Celebration of the Journey

Death, from the new paradigm, is redefined. It is the continuation of your journey of your *Self*. It is a moment to experience the dimension of your physical reality for what it is—an access to the journey of your *Self*. A brief moment where you get to experience your *Self* as who you are and bring more of your *Self* to a physical dimension where you impact the whole. In this journey you are One with All. You are within the experience of this Oneness, and it is in this experience that you come alive as your true *Self*.

From your *Mind*, your relationship to someone who died is given by your experiences with them, the *Mind's* views, thoughts, and opinions about who they were. From your *Mind* to their *Mind* there is the good, the bad, and the ugly. From your *Self*, you are only relating to that person from the journey that they chose to experience. They could be one-year-olds, twenty-year-olds, forty-year-olds, or hundred-year-olds—there is no time or linearity in their Death. There is only each moment that they were here, and the experience and gift of their being here for us and the planet.

Given this context, what honors someone is to celebrate their journey. To honor who they were and what they were about, as their *Self*. In the current paradigm, while there is what you say and do, it is always inside of the *Mind's* energy of an end and a loss and they are gone forever. Even though you know intellectually that this is not so, the vibration being emitted creates the experience for you of a loss and of never again having them with you, as the reality.

It is only when you release and transcend this truth that you will be in the experience of who they are, as a spiritual being on a spiritual journey, and what they brought forth to your life and life in general in their choice to be here in a physical form for the planet and for their journey.

From the new paradigm any sorrow or feeling of loss is your experience to transcend. Those who have passed on are in the unfolding of their journey; they are simply not in a *Body* any longer. For our journey is never about the physical plane, it is and always will be about our *Self*. When a loved one dies, those who are left behind, here in their physical form, will be in the experience of loss, sadness, despair, hopelessness, and a perception of the end, all of what the *Mind* creates as the truth. It is in this experience that you can Connect, Listen, Trust, and Act on what there is for you to know about what is occurring for you in your journey with them. For it is your journey to keep transcending your *Mind*, to Trust and Act from your *Self*. Death is a moment of great clarity as you shift from the current paradigm to the new paradigm of who you are and what your journey is about. It is in this duality, where your *Mind* is powerfully at play, that you can get access to the depth of your *Self*. It is in the moment of Death that you bring forth a deep awareness of your true *Self*, of the journey of your duality and of your access to transcending the *Mind's* truth of fear and sorrow as a reality.

The experience of Death is part of your journey, and as such it is here to impact your journey in the physical dimension. Death is the step in your journey where your *Mind* stops. It is where the role of the *Mind* is no longer a dimension of your reality. It is where you can claim that there is something beyond the physical. It is the "knowing," as you move through your life, that Death is a part of life and will be what you will go through no matter what. Just like conception, it is a part of the journey. We all experience Death no matter who you are, what your life situation and circumstances are, or how much or little you had in life. If you were poor or rich, good or bad, whatever your socioeconomic situation, the role you had in life—all of life comes to the same place for each person— in the moment of Death you are once again simply returned to energy. In this moment, it is only what you chose to honor and know about your *Self* that vibrates most powerfully. It is what makes the most sense in your journey. It is where your truth lives. It is where you see the light about all of it. It is where you resonate in the "knowing" that the physical realm is not who you are— and in that moment you know you are more than what the *Mind* has said you are, and the journey the *Mind* has played out as your truth. In that awareness you become Connected to your divine *Self*.

## Jeff, Chief Visual Director of a Video Production Company

When my father got sick with cancer, obviously as it is for any family, it was a very difficult time to go through. My father had gotten esophageal cancer in 2011. He had it removed, and we thought he had a clean bill of health, but in the summer of 2012, my father was diagnosed with Stage-4 lung cancer. The esophageal cancer cells had jumped into his lungs. And we knew it was terminal; we just didn't know how long he had. For me, my whole life I've been terribly frightened of Death and losing people and everything like that. For as long as I can remember, I've always related to it like my mom and my dad were both going to be around forever, and that anytime I needed him, I could go to my dad and he would help me out with whatever it was. When he got sick with cancer the second time, and I had to really start to deal with that, I had no idea how much more time I was going to have him around—that was terrifying. I was really scared that suddenly this safety net that I had created in my *Mind* was going to be pulled out from underneath me and I was going to be terribly alone. I didn't know what to do with it. I knew if I just listened to my *Mind* I was going to dig myself deeper and deeper into this depressing hole. So I literally had to go to Connecting because I had no other place to go. There was no release or relief anywhere else. So I started to Connect a lot. At first I got simple messages from my *Self* like, "you'll be okay," and things like that. But then I had this Connection in which I actually saw my dad passed over to the other side and he was happy, he was at peace. I had a vision of him, and he looked like he had looked in his twenties and he was on a hill and looking out over this beautiful pasture full of all kinds of animals, like deer and elk, and he looked so at peace. And for the first time in my life I experienced that my fear of Death and dying and of losing my father start to dissipate. What I got was to Trust my *Self* to say what there was to say to my father, and my mother and my sister, as they were dealing with all of this in their own way. I got in my Connection that I should tell my father that I was going to be okay and that my mom and sister were going to be okay, and that I would do whatever it took to make sure we would be okay. I Trusted that I needed to let him know that we would be okay in order for him to be at peace and not worry about us. So the Actions I took were simply when I would go over to visit him—and I did so frequently—I would take time to sit with him, to literally lie next to him and hold his hand. To experience for myself and let him know how much he was loved. My father completely shut down when he got the diagnosis from the doctor; he stopped for the most part communicating with us. Not that he didn't speak at all, but he wouldn't talk about the diagnosis or his feelings about it or anything like that. I'm a very touchy-feely kind of person, so for me I was having to deal with that he wasn't going to be that way. I realized that my father had to experience and do it the way that he felt that he had to do it. My mom wanted him to rally and be strong, and my sister wanted him to hang on and fight this to survive, and I wasn't in the same space. I knew very clearly that he was going to pass, and I Trusted that with whatever time left I had to be with him, I wanted to be my *Self* with him, and I wanted him to be allowed to be his *Self* with me. That's all I kept getting in my Connections,

*(continued)*

and to keep Trusting in that, and that I would get the Actions to take naturally when I was with him. In the end, near to my father's time of passing I clearly got in a Connection that my father was waiting for my mother to tell him that it was okay for him to go. I had a conversation with my dad, when I was alone with him, and I said, "Listen, I know you have to go, and I love you, and I just want you to know that Mom and Jennifer and I are all going to be okay, I promise you we'll be okay." I remember he looked at me kind of startled, because mainly when I was with him, we were just silent, and from the chemo and pain meds and everything, he was exhausted and kind of out of it and he didn't really react to many things, but he looked at me this time very clearly, and I got that he got it. Now up until this point I was terrified to tell my mom, "you gotta let Dad go," because from my *Mind* it was like "you can't do that, this is her spouse and she loves him and it will upset her." But from my *Self* I got, "it's okay to tell her to let him go." The next day when I was visiting, and this was the day before he passed, I had a conversation with my mom and I shared with her. I told her about my experience of seeing my father passed over and that he was at peace, and I said to her, "Listen, Mom, I know this is the hardest thing, and I want you to know that I'm always going to be here for you, and I know you don't know what to say, but I know he's waiting for you to let him go." For the first time she looked at me and said, "Do you really think so?" and I said, "I really do think so." The next evening, I got that she had let him go and he passed that day. I wasn't there, but I was actually okay with that. I didn't think I was going to be; I thought I wanted to be there to be with him when he passed, but I didn't have to be there and I was still at peace with it. I just got that I was going to be okay in life, and my mother was going to be okay in life and my sister was going to be okay in life and my father was going to be at peace. While I did grieve for my dad and I still mourn his passing, there was also a part of me that celebrated his life and his journey and his time with me. Afterward, my sister and I helped my mother put together just an amazing memorial service, which all I can tell you is that everyone kept coming up to me during it and telling me, "I've never been to a funeral like this, I feel like I got to know your father in a new way, this is such a celebration, I don't feel like I'm at a funeral." During the whole thing, I just kept getting to honor my father deeply, honor my sister and my mother, and speak from my *Self*, speak from my heart and that's all I kept doing.

## How Embracing Death Is the Access to Living a New Paradigm

Death, as an energy, is not a dimension of the Mind. To have Death vibrate as a truth from the Mind is an opposing energy to the Mind's paradigm. From the current paradigm, if you lived each moment in the embracing of your Death, you would not be living life. The experience from your Mind will evoke the emotions of how the Mind houses Death—the end, hopeless, sad, disappointment, loss, bad versus good, leaving your loved ones, and ultimately no longer existing.

Death as an energy from your Self gives you a powerful access to living in the new paradigm. Bringing forth the awareness of life as an eternal journey and that your physical form is a vehicle for this experience of your Self allows you to hold Death as a dimension of who you are in each moment. It allows you to have the experience of Death be a part of your journey and allows you to have this vibration of Death be a source for your life's journey.

In the "knowing" that Death is a real part of your choice to be here, as energy, you have a tool for holding the duality. It allows you to relate to the physical world as a gift. It allows you to know that you are not of the physical world but here to bring your *Self* to it. It allows you to presence your *Self* as your truth. It allows you to "see" those you love in the duality and to know their *Self* is also energy and also eternal. It allows you to shift the context of your life, in any moment of "now," from your *Mind* to your *Self*. It brings the totality of the journey forth as a journey. It allows the *Mind* to be a tool for the journey. It gives you a powerful access to your *Self*, and from there you can engage in the truth that you embody and experience the gift of life. You can be in the joy of it all, while holding the fear of the *Mind*. You can seek into your "knowing" for all that is happening in the physical realm. You can experience your *Self*, its magnificence and its splendor. Death, as an energy in the new paradigm, is the unfolding of the journey from the beginning. You live in a state on honoring Death as a continuation of the journey.

From your *Self*, the energy of Death is a journey to Connect, Listen, Trust, and Act to discover what there is to know about your journey. What is there to know about leaving your physical form? What is there to know about the journey you unfolded? What is there to know about the Actions to be in as you embrace the journey of leaving your physical form? I like to use this phrase, "leaving your physical form," as the word Death has a lot of energy around it from the current paradigm.

When you Connect to the statements above, you begin to shape your journey as you leave your *Body*. You begin to bring forth an awareness that deepens your Connection to your *Self* as your reality. You embrace your life and your journey for what you have unfolded, for where you lived from your *Mind* as your reality, distinct from your *Self* as your reality. You leave in the "knowing" of your true *Self*, and in doing so, you transcend the "karmic energies" and "set-up" that typically keep you disconnected from your True and Highest *Self*.

In the energy of your *Self* as your only reality, you embrace your leaving as a dimension of your *Self*, and you are within the deep love and compassion for what it means to be a human being and live in the duality. You presence the love for your *Self*, the honor for your *Self*, and the "knowing" that resonates within as your journey continues to manifest beyond the physical dimension. You can hold the *Mind* as a tool and allow yourself to release all of the truths that dishonor who you are, and in so doing leave with the "knowing" of who you are and why you are here.

## How You Can Transcend the Energy, from the *Mind*, of Death

The *Mind's* paradigm is very powerful in relating to Death as an energy of the end. There is no longer a physical form to who you know that person as, and therefore the *Mind* relates to Death as an ending of the existence of that person. While you have brought forth a "knowing" that this is not true, from the Mind it vibrates as true, and as such *is* your reality.

As you transcend this paradigm by living your life from the energy and vibration of your *Self* as who you are, having your Actions in life come from your *Self* not your *Mind*, you bring forth a new awareness of your life. You experience life as your eternal journey and you live in the "knowing" that those around you are here in a "set-up" for the journey you chose to unfold. You begin to bring another vibration to your journey with those around you. You embrace who they are in your journey by having your Actions with them come from your *Self*. As you hold the energy of Death as a dimension of your journey, your vibration evokes your being with your loved ones, void of the *Mind's* truth—that your relationships are only shaped by the physical realm. This vibration emits a truth that allows them to relate to you, not from their *Mind*, but from their *Self*.

Your transcending the fear of Death from your *Mind* reshapes how they occur for you. You "see" them as an eternal energy. You hold their energy as the duality. You honor their *Self* from your *Self*. You continue to transcend the knowing of the *Mind* to the "knowing" of your *Self*, and you release the fears that arise from your *Mind's* truth of the terror of not being in a physical form. Your journey with those around you develops a richness and a "knowing" that vibrates in the eternal nature of your journey, providing a peace and a harmony in your relationships.

# YOU: Living Your Journey Now

You have now opened up a new paradigm to live your life from. You now have an experience of your *Self* as distinct from your *Mind*. You can now begin to unfold your life from your *Self* and discover the "knowing" of your truth no matter what you are dealing with in your life. You can access the answers that are unique to you as you Connect, Listen, Trust, and Act from your *Self*.

The following is a guide to begin Connecting to your *Self* to unfold areas of your life from a new paradigm.

To begin with, know that where you are in your journey is perfect—no matter what your *Mind* thinks about your life and what is happening! Your first step is to create that everything in your life "is as it needs to be" and "All is *well*." This will take really letting go that anything is wrong. Breathe and release the concerns and worries that are there for you. Know that you will move through these concerns and worries as you practice the steps of Connecting, Listening, Trusting, and Acting.

Remember, Connecting is *not* about fixing anything in your life. It is about unfolding your journey from your *Self*. You probably have areas of your life that are going great. In those areas you want to Connect to "what there is for me to know about my journey in X area, from my *Self*, now." It is always about walking your life's journey from your *Self*.

You may be asking yourself, "How do I begin from where I am now in my life?" So I have created some starting points, given your life's circumstances and challenges. If your thoughts about the areas I have laid out below do not match your *Mind's* thoughts, then just listen for what your *Mind* says about the area when it gets difficult, hard, or upsetting. Write down whatever you get. If the area is working well, then Connect for what there is to know in this moment of "now." Read the ones that apply to you for guidance in getting the answers that are unique to you. I have created several different scenarios with some possible *Mind* thoughts that could be there.

Do the recommended Connections and write down everything you get exactly the way you get it. You may get colors, images, or words. It doesn't have to look any particular way. If you didn't get anything in the Connection (the *Mind* is blocking), then answer the question when you open your eyes. After that circle the words that you can see have a softer vibration that could be from your *Self*. With practice, you will be able to tell the difference. The language of *Self* does not use words like "should," "have to," or "need to." Your *Self* is there as a guide, and as such it speaks more softly.

You will end up in one of three places out of your Connections:

1.  Your Connection and what you got was from the *Mind*. This is not a problem even if you take your actions from the *Mind* because you are mostly operating from there in your life anyway. However, the

sheer act of Connecting opens up your access to your *Self*. You have altered your vibration, and now it is only a matter of time before the words from your *Self will* come through.

2.  Your Connection has some *Self* and some *Mind*. The actions you take will create a different impact in your life, even the actions from your *Mind*.

3.  Your Connection is from your *Self*. You are now in Action in life, living the journey You came to live and experience. You will experience a shift in how this area resonates for you as you open up a new pathway to resolving how this area unfolds. This is the true joy of life.

## Possible Life Situations to Connect To

*You as a Single Person Looking for a Partner*

The *Mind's* energy: Your *Mind* has identified all of your flaws and focuses on the things you need to change in order to be attractive to someone. You may or may not have confidence in who you are, which has been formulated by your *Mind* from past decisions about you, people, and situations. Either way, this leaves you in some sort of concern from your *Mind* about finding someone who wants you for you. The energy of your *Self* is vibrant, centered in the gift you are for life.

Connect to: "What is there for me to know about being in a relationship, now, from my *Self*?" Given what you get in this Connection, Connect to: "What actions am I to be in, now?" Web link: www.indiratoday.com/single

## You as a Single Parent

The *Mind's* energy: You may think that you are now limited and trapped by your circumstances. How can you ever find love again? Your *Mind* may not even care about a relationship now. Your *Mind's* thoughts make up and limit your view of your journey and life. Your constant attention is around trying to balance and juggle the circumstances. From the *Mind*, it does not look like this is how your life "should" look. The weeks, months, years pass with no real light at the end of the tunnel. "What is it all really about?" is running through your *Mind*.

> Connect to: "What is there for me to know about being my *Self* with my children/child, now?" "What is there for me to know about my journey with (name of ex-spouse, child/children's father), from my *Self*?" "What is there for me to know about being in a relationship from my *Self* at this time?" Given what you get in those connections, Connect to: "What actions am I to be in, now?" Web link: www. indiratoday.com/singleparent

## You as a Spouse

The *Mind's* energy: In the beginning of all personal relationships, there is an experience of excitement, and then the *Mind* starts to go to work to find the other person's flaws—all of the things that don't work about them. It will create circumstances and situations to keep heightening and repeating the flaws. The *Mind* will try to fix the other person or tolerate the flaw. This can generate a low-level energy of annoyance or a high-level energy of being upset. Either way it is your "karmic energies" kicking in, and it has nothing to do with your spouse. They are playing out a role your *Mind* has "set up." What cannot be seen is that you are together for your journey with each other in this lifetime. You are a gift to each other to transcend the *Mind's* energies and triggers, for the opportunity of the journey of your *Selves* together.

Connect to: "What is there for me to know about being my *Self* in my journey with (spouse's/partner name), at this time?" "What is there for me to know about honoring (name of spouse/partner), from my *Self*?" Given what you get in those connections, Connect to: "What actions am I to be in, now?" Web link: www.indiratoday.com/couple

*You as a Parent*

The *Mind's* energy: Your focus has moved to the children as the center of your relationship. It becomes your primary focus and attention. You may even experience a distance being created in your relationship with your spouse/partner. The demands of the family become the driving force in life. Each of the family members will bring up uniquely different "karmic energies" from the *Mind* for you to transcend. The gift of them being in your life is to powerfully discover your *Self* and experience the joy of your life through your journey with them from your *Self*.

Connect to: "What is there for me to know about being my *Self* in my journey with my children(can list each name child), now? "What is there for me to know about being my *Self* in my journey with (spouse's/partner name), at this time?" Given what you get in those connections, Connect to: "What actions am I to be in, now?" Web link: www. indiratoday.com/parent

*You as a Manager/Executive/Business Owner*

The *Mind's* energy: If you operate from your *Mind's* energies, your career will be filled with hard work, concerns, worries, and upsets. In any management position, there are people you get along with well, some not so well, and some you avoid. These categories are all from your *Mind*. All of the beliefs you have about each person, the company, and any situation are all the "karmic energies" you have "set up" to transcend to discover your *Self* and make the impact in the world you came to make. You do not have to worry or be concerned about moving ahead. Your life will unfold consistent with your intentions, your journey, and your impact in the world provided you are Connecting, Listening, Trusting, and Acting from your *Self*.

> Connect to: "What is there for me to know about my journey with (name of company) from my *Self*, now?" "What is there for me to know about being my *Self* in my journey as a manager, now?" "What is there for me to know from my *Self* about my journey as a manager with my team/employees, now?" Given what you get in those connections, Connect to: "What actions am I to be in?" Web link: www.indiratoday.com/manager

*You as an Employee*

The *Mind's* energy: You are working to make a living. It could be satisfying or simply a routine you are in. The *Mind* will have comments about everything happening. The thought of "What is it really all about?" slips in. Days, weeks, months pass as you are in life doing what your *Mind* tells you that you should be doing, while wondering, "Am I doing everything I should be doing?"

Connect to: "What is there for me to know from my *Self* about my journey in life, now?" "What is there for me to know about unfolding my journey with (name of company) from my *Self* now?" Given what you get in those connections, Connect to: "What actions am I to be in, now?" Web link: www.indiratoday.com/employee

### You as a Sibling

The *Mind's* energy: You may be in communication with your brothers and sisters frequently, infrequently, or not at all. Your *Mind* has made up a lot about them from the events and situations that have happened in your journey with them. Consider that all of what has happened was designed by your *Mind* to evoke the relationship you have with your siblings. The *Mind's* energy could be really strong about its beliefs about them. Consider that you came into this life to transcend these energies as a way of accessing your *Self*. Even if you have a great relationship, it is about being with them to discover more about your *Self*.

Connect to: "What is there for me to know about being my *Self* now in my journey with (name of siblings)?" Given what you get in those connections, Connect to: "What actions am I to be in, now?" Web link: www.indiratoday.com/sibling

### You as a Daughter or Son

The *Mind's* energy: Our parents were our choice. The *Mind* does not want you to relate to this as true. It will have a lot to say about who they weren't for you or what was wrong in your relationship. You picked them so that you could have the life you have with all of what has happened to you so that you can transcend the *Mind's* energies in the discovery of your *Self*. Even if you have a great relationship with your parents, it is still about moving through the *Mind's* energies about them and life.

Connect to: "What is there for me to know about being my *Self* in my journey with my parents?" Given what you get in those connections, Connect to: "What actions am I to be in, now?" Web link: www.indiratoday.com/daughter-son

*You and Your Life's Purpose*

The *Mind's* energy: The *Mind* has your "life's purpose" as a place to end up. The *Mind* is always trying to get somewhere. It is driven to have life be a race. When you are so consumed about getting somewhere, you cannot see what is in front of you if it isn't related to where the *Mind* thinks you should go. It is hard for the *Mind* to get there is nothing to do. From your *Self* there is only what is unfolding in this moment of "now," then this moment of "now," etc. When you can stay this present to life, you will see the pathways from your *Self* to step into. It is about Connecting to all of the events and situations that arise in your life. When your actions are coming from Connecting to your *Self*, you are naturally fulfilling your purpose and impact in the world. Choose a few of the situations occurring around you that pull you away from being yourself.

Connect to: "What is there for me to know about unfolding my journey from my *Self* in this situation/event/person), now?" Given what you get in those connections, Connect to: "What actions am I to be in, now?" Web link: www.indiratoday.com/purpose

Here are other areas you can Connect to depending on your circumstances now:

- You as a worker/manager/executive who lost their job

- You as a person who has been out of work for a long time

- You in an experience of being trapped in a relationship or job

- You as a widowed spouse

- You as a person at risk (incarcerated, drugs, substance abuse)

- You as a young adult living at home

Remember everything that is happening is all part of the journey of your *Self*. Given this, you would want to be guided, from your *Self*, for what there is for you to know. You can Connect to anything that is occurring for you in life—a situation, a person, an event, a gathering. Consider your life as a moment-by-moment unfolding of your journey. You came here for this gift.

Have a lot of compassion for being a human being whose only reality has been shaped by the *Mind*. In living from this paradigm of *Self*, you may experience feeling like a baby learning to walk and talk—it is a new way of "walking" your life as You. It is the recognition that what vibrates within you is your *Self*.

For me, my life is only about having my actions come from my *Self*. I spend my days disengaging where my *Mind* has taken control and continuing to Connect, Listen, Trust, and Act from my *Self*. I am clear that by doing this in my life all of my relationships, having the health that assures honoring my *Body*, experiencing the love of myself, honoring the *Self* of those around me, and unfolding my best life are guaranteed.

I see the world through the lens of the journey of who we are as a collective vibration of *Self*. I transcend the fears that are evoked as the *Mind* reacts to what is happening or not happening in the world around me. I am at peace in a new state of living from "all is well," "all is as it should be," as I Connect for what Actions I am to be in about any and all situations where there is a concern or worry. This is a peace that can never be known from my *Mind*. I continue to disengage the needs and wants of my *Mind* as I Trust unconditionally what I get to Act on from my *Self*. I live within bringing my *Self* to life as I confront and transcend the pull of the *Mind* to keep me contained and separate from being all of Me. I know that by living from my *Self* as who I am, I will take my last breath in the "knowing" of who I am and why I chose to be in a physical form.

This is all available to you now.

The website www.indiratoday.com contains many tools you can use to develop the muscle of walking your journey from *Self* and strengthening Listening to your *Self* as naturally and effortlessly as you do your *Mind*.

### Living the Journey of Your Life from *Self*

So how do you begin to live from your *Self* as a way of living your life? Here are the structures to support you in living from this new paradigm of *Self*.

1. Set up a place in your home where you can Connect. To Connect requires a quiet place, so choose a specific place such as your bedroom or another serene room in

the house where you can disengage the world around you. Having a place where you will Connect makes a big difference as it sets up the *Mind* to know that you are choosing to Connect as a way of living. It makes it easier for the *Mind* to allow Connecting to become a part of your daily and weekly routine.

2. Download the Connection mp3 from my website to use when you Connect. In the beginning this will be a guide for you in unplugging the *Mind*. To disengage the *Mind* will take effort and time. Using the guided Connection will support you in shifting the *Mind's* vibration of total control where the intuitive *Self* can become more available to you as you develop your ability to Connect to *Self* on demand. To download the mp3, go to www.indiratoday.com/book/connect.

3. Have a journal where you can write down what you get from your Connections. The moment you come out of your Connection the *Mind* is right there to take control again, so writing down whatever arose for you immediately is very important as you begin learning to tell the difference between the *Mind* and *Self*.

4. Take the Actions you get from your *Self*. Put them on your calendar or in your day planner. Given the *Mind's* control of life, taking the Actions you got from your *Self* will not be on your radar, so having a specific structure to remind you is the key to taking the Actions.

5. Use this book as a guide to keep learning about the *Mind* and *Self*. Highlight where you experience seeing the realm of the *Mind* and the realm of *Self* so you can go back and reread it over and over again.

6. Keep checking my website www.indiratoday.com to download tools and read other's experiences of Connecting. This is a structure I created to support you in Connecting, Listening, Trusting, and Acting from your *Self* as a way of living your life.

# As You Embark on Your Journey

Like any new practice it takes time and patience to embrace a way of living life. Living from your *Self* is like going to the gym and practicing to lift a two-pound weight and then a five-pound weight . . . pretty soon you are surprised at how strong you have become.

Such is Connecting, Listening, Trusting, and Acting. Have a lot of patience and compassion with yourself. The *Mind* will want to take over, but use all of the resources available to you through the tools in this book and the website as well as being in communication with me through the website.

In the beginning as you develop your Connecting and the messages you get, do not worry about trying to figure out what is coming from your *Mind* and what is coming from your *Self*. As I said earlier, the vibrational difference will become clear to you in time.

You are on an incredible journey. You will discover and access your *Self* for who you are in many areas of your life.

All of what is said in this book is available to you from your *Self*. What led you to this book is your *Self*. Embrace this You. It is there within you, the You of your *Self*.

As you embark on this remarkable journey of knowing your *Self*, I am there with you in *Spirit*. As a force of energy, I honor who you are and why you are here. I know that you will bring forth all of what you wish for in living your true *Self*.

I wish you many blessings on this remarkable journey of living from your *Self*, as you unfold who you are and why you are here for your family, friends, and the planet.

With Love,
Indira

# Glossary

**Activate**   To bring the vibration of energy to life as real.

**Awareness**   Being able to see and observe the *Mind* and what it is saying without relating to it as You

**Conception**   The moment of choice to be in a physical form.

**Connect**   Accessing the communication from your *Self* by unplugging the *Mind*.

**Duality**   Having both the *Mind* and *Self* available to you in any moment.

**Energy**   A force of vibration and resonance that flows through all things.

**Eternal Nature**   The totality of who you are as a force of divine energy.

**Frequency**   The rhythm in which something moves.

**Happening**   A declaration you make before or after a situation that marks it as something to Connect to for what there is to know from *Self*.

**Journey**   Relating to your life as a flow of events that are unfolding a pathway your *Self* came to experience.

**Karmic Energy**   An energy from your past (this or other lifetimes) that creates some reaction within you, that throws you into a patterned role that the *Mind* operates from as real.

**Knowing/Inner Knowing**   The communication from the eternal *Self* that dwells within you.

**Manifest/Manifestation**   Allowing something to be created in the physical world from energy as our only reality.

**Mind**   The constant flow of thoughts about everything; it is a mechanical device that is related only to the physical world.

**Moment of "Now"**   The moment of no *Mind*, allowing for the totality of *Self* to presence itself; in this instant is a new moment from which to create a new experience of life from the energy and vibration for the eternal *Self*.

**Paradigm**   A theoretical framework that gives us the way we see, act, and be in the world. It gives us what we say, how we think; it creates a reality of how people, situations, events, and the world are. It is the box inside of which you operate.

**Presence/Presencing**   The moment that energy is experienced.

**Purpose**   What your life is for and its impact in the world that arises as your actions in each moment of "now" comes from your *Self*.

**Resonate/Resonance**   When something "rings true" at a cellular level.

**Seek into**   Stopping the action of life and creating the awareness of or looking deeper into what is going on in an area of life or a situation from your journey as energy.

**Self**   The intuitive part of you; the Spirit you are; the life force within you.

**Set-up**   Seeing the relationships and events around us for how our *Mind* gets triggered, giving us an opening to presence our *Self*.

**Transcend**   Shifting energy that is evoked by the Mind, such that it no longer reactivates you.

**Triggered**   The setting off of an automatic response from the *Mind's* energy.

**Universal Energy/Universal Consciousness**   The speaking of divine energy at its origin.

**Vibrate**   The energetic movement that allows something to exist.

**Vow**   A decision from the *Mind* that creates a truth about who you are as a reality.

# Acknowledgments

First I want to thank all of those individuals who have been with me along this journey; my guides and my dear and loving friends. You all know who are.

I am thankful to my partner and husband, Paul for the endless time spent reviewing the content assuring its readability and flow, and your contribution in the writing of the YOU chapter and the glossary. Thank you for your love, your heart, and your eternal spirit.

I am very thankful to Donna Clapp, whose editorial expertise really helped the flow and content. Your commitment to having this book published was a force in making it happen.

Deep gratitude to Jeff Clapp for his creativity in producing the book cover.

Thank you to Ramonita Santiago for her support and contributions.

To my Mom, Dad, sisters, and brothers, you are my foundation. Thank you for always allowing me to be my *Self*, even if it sometimes made no sense, and for loving me unconditionally. The greatest gift I have in my life is your love.

# About the Author

 Indira Dyal-Dominguez has delivered programs on guiding others to be their true *Self* for more than twenty years. Through years of meditation, rebirthing, self-healing, and experiencing herself and others as a force of energy, Indira has brought forth the ability to Connect to her inner *Self* and teach others to do the same. Through her workshops, individual and group programs, and the corporate seminars she developed with her husband, Paul, Indira has personally coached and trained thousands of people, giving them access to pursue and fulfill their purpose and their dreams. Indira's passion is making a difference in the lives of others. Knowing that she has contributed to another human being is what brings her the most joy in life.

www.indiratoday.com